GENERAL EDITORS

Dale C. Garell, M.D.
Medical Director, California Children Services, Department of Health
  Services, County of Los Angeles
Clinical Professor, Department of Pediatrics & Family Medicine,
  University of Southern California School of Medicine
Former president, Society for Adolescent Medicine

Solomon H. Snyder, M.D.
Distinguished Service Professor of Neuroscience, Pharmacology, and
  Psychiatry, Johns Hopkins University School of Medicine
Former president, Society of Neuroscience
Albert Lasker Award in Medical Research, 1978

CONSULTING EDITORS

Robert W. Blum, M.D., Ph.D.
Associate Professor, School of Public Health and Department of
  Pediatrics
Director, Adolescent Health Program, University of Minnesota
Consultant, World Health Organization

Charles E. Irwin, Jr., M.D.
Associate Professor of Pediatrics
Director, Division of Adolescent Medicine,
  University of California, San Francisco

Lloyd J. Kolbe, Ph.D.
Chief, Office of School Health & Special Projects, Center for Health
  Promotion & Education, Centers for Disease Control
President, American School Health Association

Jordan J. Popkin
Director, Division of Federal Employee Occupational Health, U.S. Public
  Health Service Region I

Joseph L. Rauh, M.D.
Professor of Pediatrics and Medicine, Adolescent Medicine, Children's
  Hospital Medical Center, Cincinnati
Former president, Society for Adolescent Medicine

THE ENCYCLOPEDIA OF
HEALTH

MEDICAL DISORDERS
AND THEIR TREATMENT

Dale C. Garell, M.D. · General Editor

MONONUCLEOSIS AND OTHER INFECTIOUS DISEASES

Laurel Shader, M.D.,
and Jon Zonderman

Introduction by C. Everett Koop, M.D., Sc.D.
Surgeon General, U.S. Public Health Service

08/27/90   18.95

608048   08555

CHELSEA HOUSE PUBLISHERS
New York · Philadelphia

The goal of the ENCYCLOPEDIA OF HEALTH *is to provide general information in the ever-changing areas of physiology, psychology, and related medical issues. The titles in this series are not intended to take the place of the professional advice of a physician or other health-care professional.*

Chelsea House Publishers
EDITOR-IN-CHIEF Nancy Toff
EXECUTIVE EDITOR Remmel T. Nunn
MANAGING EDITOR Karyn Gullen Browne
COPY CHIEF Juliann Barbato
PICTURE EDITOR Adrian G. Allen
ART DIRECTOR Maria Epes
MANUFACTURING MANAGER Gerald Levine

The Encyclopedia of Health
SENIOR EDITOR Paula Edelson

Staff for MONONUCLEOSIS AND OTHER INFECTIOUS DISEASES
ASSISTANT EDITOR James M. Cornelius
DEPUTY COPY CHIEF Nicole Bowen
EDITORIAL ASSISTANT Jennifer Trachtenberg
PICTURE RESEARCHER Sandy Jones
ASSISTANT ART DIRECTOR Loraine Machlin
SENIOR DESIGNER Marjorie Zaum
LAYOUT Bernard Schliefer
PRODUCTION COORDINATOR Joseph Romano

Copyright © 1989 by Chelsea House Publishers, a division of Main Line Book Co. All rights reserved. Printed and bound in the United States of America.

3 5 7 9 8 6 4 2

Library of Congress Cataloging-in-Publication Data

Shader, Laurel.
  Mononucleosis and other infectious diseases / Laurel Shader and Jon Zonderman; introduction by C. Everett Koop.
  p. cm.—(The Encyclopedia of health. Medical disorders and their treatment)
  Bibliography: p.
  Includes index.
  Summary: Examines various infectious diseases, including mononucleosis, chicken pox, and infections of the respiratory, gastrointestinal, and genitourinary systems.
  ISBN 0-7910-0069-9—
      0-7910-0496-1 (pbk.)
  1. Communicable diseases—Juvenile literature. 2. Mononucleosis—Juvenile literature. [1. Communicable diseases. 2. Diseases.]
  I. Zonderman, Jon. II. Title. III. Series.   88-34186
  RC113.S48 1989   CIP
  616.9—dc 19   AC

CONTENTS

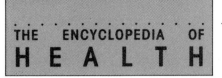

THE ENCYCLOPEDIA OF
HEALTH

THE HEALTHY BODY

The Circulatory System
Dental Health
The Digestive System
The Endocrine System
Exercise
Genetics & Heredity
The Human Body: An Overview
Hygiene
The Immune System
Memory & Learning
The Musculoskeletal System
The Neurological System
Nutrition
The Reproductive System
The Respiratory System
The Senses
Speech & Hearing
Sports Medicine
Vision
Vitamins & Minerals

THE LIFE CYCLE

Adolescence
Adulthood
Aging
Childhood
Death & Dying
The Family
Friendship & Love
Pregnancy & Birth

MEDICAL ISSUES

Careers in Health Care
Environmental Health
Folk Medicine
Health Care Delivery
Holistic Medicine
Medical Ethics
Medical Fakes & Frauds
Medical Technology
Medicine & the Law
Occupational Health
Public Health

PSYCHOLOGICAL DISORDERS AND THEIR TREATMENT

Anxiety & Phobias
Child Abuse
Compulsive Behavior
Delinquency & Criminal Behavior
Depression
Diagnosing & Treating Mental Illness
Eating Habits & Disorders
Learning Disabilities
Mental Retardation
Personality Disorders
Schizophrenia
Stress Management
Suicide

MEDICAL DISORDERS AND THEIR TREATMENT

AIDS
Allergies
Alzheimer's Disease
Arthritis
Birth Defects
Cancer
The Common Cold
Diabetes
First Aid & Emergency Medicine
Gynecological Disorders
Headaches
The Hospital
Kidney Disorders
Medical Diagnosis
The Mind-Body Connection
Mononucleosis and Other Infectious Diseases
Nuclear Medicine
Organ Transplants
Pain
Physical Handicaps
Poisons & Toxins
Prescription & OTC Drugs
Sexually Transmitted Diseases
Skin Disorders
Stroke & Heart Disease
Substance Abuse
Tropical Medicine

PREVENTION AND EDUCATION: THE KEYS TO GOOD HEALTH

C. Everett Koop, M.D., Sc.D.
Surgeon General,
U.S. Public Health Service

The issue of health education has received particular attention in recent years because of the presence of AIDS in the news. But our response to this particular tragedy points up a number of broader issues that doctors, public health officials, educators, and the public face. In particular, it points up the necessity for sound health education for citizens of all ages.

Over the past 25 years this country has been able to bring about dramatic declines in the death rates for heart disease, stroke, accidents, and, for people under the age of 45, cancer. Today, Americans generally eat better and take better care of themselves than ever before. Thus, with the help of modern science and technology, they have a better chance of surviving serious—even catastrophic—illnesses. That's the good news.

But, like every phonograph record, there's a flip side, and one with special significance for young adults. According to a report issued in 1979 by Dr. Julius Richmond, my predecessor as Surgeon General, Americans aged 15 to 24 had a higher death rate in 1979 than they did 20 years earlier. The causes: violent death and injury, alcohol and drug abuse, unwanted pregnancies, and sexually transmitted diseases. Adolescents are particularly vulnerable, because they are beginning to explore their own sexuality and perhaps to experiment with drugs. The need for educating young people is critical, and the price of neglect is high.

Yet even for the population as a whole, our health is still far from what it could be. Why? A 1974 Canadian government report attributed all death and disease to four broad elements: inadequacies in the health-care system, behavioral factors or unhealthy life-styles, environmental hazards, and human biological factors.

To be sure, there are diseases that are still beyond the control of even our advanced medical knowledge and techniques. And despite yearnings that are as old as the human race itself, there is no "fountain of youth" to ward off aging and death. Still, there is a solution to many of the problems that undermine sound health. In a word, that solution is prevention. Prevention, which includes health promotion and education, saves lives, improves the quality of life, and, in the long run, saves money.

In the United States, organized public health activities and preventive medicine have a long history. Important milestones include the improvement of sanitary procedures and the development of pasteurized milk in the late 19th century, and the introduction in the mid-20th century of effective vaccines against polio, measles, German measles, mumps, and other once-rampant diseases. Internationally, organized public health efforts began on a wide-scale basis with the International Sanitary Conference of 1851, to which 12 nations sent representatives. The World Health Organization, founded in 1948, continues these efforts under the aegis of the United Nations, with particular emphasis on combatting communicable diseases and the training of health-care workers.

But despite these accomplishments, much remains to be done in the field of prevention. For too long, we have had a medical care system that is science- and technology-based, focused, essentially, on illness and mortality. It is now patently obvious that both the social and the economic costs of such a system are becoming insupportable.

Implementing prevention—and its corollaries, health education and promotion—is the job of several groups of people:

First, the medical and scientific professions need to continue basic scientific research, and here we are making considerable progress. But increased concern with prevention will also have a decided impact on how primary-care doctors practice medicine. With a shift to health-based rather than morbidity-based medicine, the role of the "new physician" will include a healthy dose of patient education.

Second, practitioners of the social and behavioral sciences—psychologists, economists, city planners—along with lawyers, business leaders, and government officials—must solve the practical and ethical dilemmas confronting us: poverty, crime, civil rights, literacy, education, employment, housing, sanitation, environmental protection, health care delivery systems, and so forth. All of these issues affect public health.

Third is the public at large. We'll consider that very important group in a moment.

Fourth, and the linchpin in this effort, is the public health profession—doctors, epidemiologists, teachers—who must harness the professional expertise of the first two groups and the common sense and cooperation of the third, the public. They must define the problems statistically and qualitatively and then help us set priorities for finding the solutions.

To a very large extent, improving those statistics is the responsibility of every individual. So let's consider more specifically what the role of the individual should be and why health education is so important to that role. First, and most obviously, individuals can protect themselves from illness and injury and thus minimize their need for professional medical care. They can eat a nutritious diet, get adequate exercise, avoid tobacco, alcohol, and drugs, and take prudent steps to avoid accidents. The proverbial "apple a day keeps the doctor away" is not so far from the truth, after all.

Second, individuals should actively participate in their own medical care. They should schedule regular medical and dental checkups. Should they develop an illness or injury, they should know when to treat themselves and when to seek professional help. To gain the maximum benefit from any medical treatment that they do require, individuals must become partners in that treatment. For instance, they should understand the effects and side effects of medications. I counsel young physicians that there is no such thing as too much information when talking with patients. But the corollary is the patient must know enough about the nuts and bolts of the healing process to understand what the doctor is telling him. That is at least partially the patient's responsibility.

Education is equally necessary for us to understand the ethical and public policy issues in health care today. Sometimes individuals will encounter these issues in making decisions about their own treatment or that of family members. Other citizens may encounter them as jurors in medical malpractice cases. But we all become involved, indirectly, when we elect our public officials, from school board members to the president. Should surrogate parenting be legal? To what extent is drug testing desirable, legal, or necessary? Should there be public funding for family planning, hospitals, various types of medical research, and medical care for the indigent? How should we allocate scant technological resources, such as kidney dialysis and organ transplants? What is the proper role of government in protecting the rights of patients?

What are the broad goals of public health in the United States today? In 1980, the Public Health Service issued a report aptly entitled *Promoting Health-Preventing Disease: Objectives for the Nation.* This report expressed its goals in terms of mortality and in terms of intermediate goals in education and health improvement. It identified 15 major concerns: controlling high blood pressure; improving family planning; improving pregnancy care and infant health; increasing the rate of immunization; controlling sexually transmitted diseases; controlling the presence of toxic agents and radiation in the environment; improving occupational safety and health; preventing accidents; promoting water fluoridation and dental health; controlling infectious diseases; decreasing smoking; decreasing alcohol and drug abuse; improving nutrition; promoting physical fitness and exercise; and controlling stress and violent behavior.

For healthy adolescents and young adults (ages 15 to 24), the specific goal was a 20% reduction in deaths, with a special focus on motor vehicle injuries and alcohol and drug abuse. For adults (ages 25 to 64), the aim was 25% fewer deaths, with a concentration on heart attacks, strokes, and cancers.

Smoking is perhaps the best example of how individual behavior can have a direct impact on health. Today cigarette smoking is recognized as the most important single preventable cause of death in our society. It is responsible for more cancers and more cancer deaths than any other known agent; is a prime risk factor for heart and blood vessel disease, chronic bronchitis, and emphysema; and is a frequent cause of complications in pregnancies and of babies born prematurely, underweight, or with potentially fatal respiratory and cardiovascular problems.

Since the release of the Surgeon General's first report on smoking in 1964, the proportion of adult smokers has declined substantially, from 43% in 1965 to 30.5% in 1985. Since 1965, 37 million people have quit smoking. Although there is still much work to be done if we are to become a "smoke-free society," it is heartening to note that public health and public education efforts—such as warnings on cigarette packages and bans on broadcast advertising—have already had significant effects.

In 1835, Alexis de Tocqueville, a French visitor to America, wrote, "In America the passion for physical well-being is general." Today, as then, health and fitness are front-page items. But with the greater scientific and technological resources now available to us, we are in a far stronger position to make good health care available to everyone. And with the greater technological threats to us as we approach the 21st century, the need to do so is more urgent than ever before. Comprehensive information about basic biology, preventive medicine, medical and surgical treatments, and related ethical and public policy issues can help you arm yourself with the knowledge you need to be healthy throughout your life.

FOREWORD

Dale C. Garell, M.D.

Advances in our understanding of health and disease during the 20th century have been truly remarkable. Indeed, it could be argued that modern health care is one of the greatest accomplishments in all of human history. In the early 1900s, improvements in sanitation, water treatment, and sewage disposal reduced death rates and increased longevity. Previously untreatable illnesses can now be managed with antibiotics, immunizations, and modern surgical techniques. Discoveries in the fields of immunology, genetic diagnosis, and organ transplantation are revolutionizing the prevention and treatment of disease. Modern medicine is even making inroads against cancer and heart disease, two of the leading causes of death in the United States.

Although there is much to be proud of, medicine continues to face enormous challenges. Science has vanquished diseases such as smallpox and polio, but new killers, most notably AIDS, confront us. Moreover, we now victimize ourselves with what some have called "diseases of choice," or those brought on by drug and alcohol abuse, bad eating habits, and mismanagement of the stresses and strains of contemporary life. The very technology that is doing so much to prolong life has brought with it previously unimaginable ethical dilemmas related to issues of death and dying. The rising cost of health-care is a matter of central concern to us all. And violence in the form of automobile accidents, homicide, and suicide remain the major killers of young adults.

In the past, most people were content to leave health care and medical treatment in the hands of professionals. But since the 1960s, the consumer of medical care—that is, the patient—has assumed an increasingly central role in the management of his or her own health. There has also been a new emphasis placed on prevention: People are recognizing that their own actions can help prevent many of the conditions that have caused death and disease in the past. This accounts for the growing commitment to good nutrition and regular exercise, for the fact that more and more people are choosing not to smoke, and for a new moderation in people's drinking habits.

People want to know more about themselves and their own health. They are curious about their body: its anatomy, physiology, and biochemistry. They want to keep up with rapidly evolving medical technologies and procedures. They are willing to educate themselves about common disorders and diseases so that they can be full partners in their own health-care.

The ENCYCLOPEDIA OF HEALTH is designed to provide the basic knowledge that readers will need if they are to take significant responsibility for their own health. It is also meant to serve as a frame of reference for further study and exploration. The ENCYCLOPEDIA is divided into five subsections: The Healthy Body; The Life Cycle; Medical Disorders & Their Treatment; Psychological Disorders & Their Treatment; and Medical Issues. For each topic covered by the ENCYCLOPEDIA, we present the essential facts about the relevant biology; the symptoms, diagnosis, and treatment of common diseases and disorders; and ways in which you can prevent or reduce the severity of health problems when that is possible. The ENCYCLOPEDIA also projects what may lie ahead in the way of future treatment or prevention strategies.

The broad range of topics and issues covered in the ENCYCLOPEDIA reflects the fact that human health encompasses physical, psychological, social, environmental, and spiritual well-being. Just as the mind and the body are inextricably linked, so, too, is the individual an integral part of the wider world that comprises his or her family, society, and environment. To discuss health in its broadest aspect it is necessary to explore the many ways in which it is connected to such fields as law, social science, public policy, economics, and even religion. And so, the ENCYCLOPEDIA is meant to be a bridge between science, medical technology, the world at large, and you. I hope that it will inspire you to pursue in greater depth particular areas of interest, and that you will take advantage of the suggestions for further reading and the lists of resources and organizations that can provide additional information.

A WORLD OF DISEASE

Mumps, 1908.

Within the world perceived through human senses—through the gifts of sight, hearing, smell, taste, and touch—exists another, hidden world. It teems with microorganisms—bacteria, viruses, and others—that constantly threaten to invade people's bodies. When they succeed, as they often do, the result is illness. Sometimes one catches a mild cold—often from an infected family member or friend—that lasts only a day or two, hardly a lengthy span but usually an uncomfortable one. One coughs, sneezes, and may run a slight fever. But recovery comes soon, and no permanent harm has been done.

Other infectious, somewhat more threatening illnesses take a greater toll. For instance, mononucleosis—an infectious disease that often strikes adolescents and young adults—causes a feeling of fatigue that can last for two months and give rise to many discomforts and some danger, as explained in Chapter 3 of this volume.

There are infectious diseases that can prove deadly. The best-known example of this in the 1980s is acquired immune deficiency syndrome (AIDS), a viral infection that has destroyed the immune systems of millions of victims worldwide, dooming them to death. As of 1989, researchers had made some important discoveries about the AIDS virus, but a cure lay a long way off.

AIDS is a new disease, but the phenomenon of the epidemic, a sudden outbreak of devastating illness, is not new at all. Indeed, history abounds in examples of epidemics that beset entire communities—cities, nations, even continents. Many of these deadly scourges are discussed in Chapter 1 of this volume, an overview of infectious diseases and the impact they have had on humankind, ancient and modern.

Until quite recently, no tools existed for rooting out the cause of diseases and controlling the devious means by which they spread. It was only in the 17th century, for instance, that people realized the crucial need for sanitary living conditions. Many of the worst epidemics could have been avoided if communities had known the value of clean streets and sewage systems.

No matter what precautions are taken, however, the hidden world of microorganisms exists, and infectious diseases continue to threaten people's bodily systems. This book describes some of the most common infectious diseases. It explains how they defeat the defenses of the human body, the symptoms that alert physicians to their presence, and the therapies that restore sound health.

·   ·   ·   ·

CHAPTER 1

· · · · · · · · · · · ·

THE
SCOURGES OF
HUMANITY

An engraving of the 6th-century A.D. plague in Rome.

A s early as the 5th century B.C., the Greek philosophers Leu-
cippus and Democritus advanced the concept of *atomism*,
which held that all matter was composed of atoms (the word
originally meant "minute indivisible particles") arranged in certain shapes. The concept received full expression in the 1st century B.C., in *De rerum natura* (The nature of things), a long poem
by the Roman poet Lucretius. He endorsed the idea that all matter, our souls, and the gods were composed of atoms, and he also
claimed that there were "seeds" of disease in the air. Thus was
born the theory that infectious diseases are caused by living par-

ticles too small to be seen with the naked eye. Nearly 2,000 years passed, however, before scientists developed tools and techniques that substantiated this remarkable intuition.

THE PLAGUE YEARS

Little as the ancients knew about the causes of disease, they accurately described its effects, especially during the gruesome plagues that sometimes cursed entire populations. In his *History of the Peloponnesian War*, written in the 5th century B.C., the Greek historian Thucydides meticulously described the symptoms of plague that devastated Athens between 430 and 428 during its war against the city of Sparta:

> . . . people in good health were all of a sudden attacked by violent heats in the head, and redness and inflammation in the eyes, the inward parts, such as the throat or tongue, becoming bloody and emitting an unnatural and fetid breath. These symptoms were followed by sneezing and hoarseness, after which the pain soon reached the chest, and produced a hard cough. When it fixed in the stomach, it upset it; and discharges of bile of every kind named by physicians ensued, accompanied by very great distress. In most cases also an ineffectual retching followed, producing violent spasms, which in some cases ceased soon after, in others much later. Externally the body was not very hot to the touch, nor pale in its appearance, but reddish, livid, and breaking out into small pustules and ulcers. But internally it burned so that the patient could not bear to have on him clothing or linen even of the lightest description; or indeed to be otherwise than stark naked.

For centuries, plague remained the scourge of Western civilization. In ancient Rome, the worst episode began in A.D. 540, when a 50-year epidemic of the bubonic plague—a horrible illness whose victims are attacked by high fever and *buboes*, swollen glands in the armpits and groin—ravaged the entire empire from North Africa and Palestine to the Mediterranean states in Europe.

A rat-patrol station, Philadelphia, 1914. Rat fleas spread the bacterium that causes one kind of plague. An infestation of rats often signals poor sanitation and can lead to an outbreak of disease.

In the early years of this epidemic—called the Plague of Justinian, after the emperor of the time—10,000 people died each day. According to English historian Edward Gibbon, author of *The History of the Decline and Fall of the Roman Empire* (1776–88), some areas of the Roman Empire never regained their population density.

There are two types of bubonic plague: classic and pneumonic. Classic plague is spread by fleas that bite humans after having themselves bitten infected rats. Because every victim must contract the ailment in this way—from a flea that has bitten a rat—classic plague spreads slowly. Pneumonic plague, however, spreads more easily. An infected person can pass on the fatal bacteria by coughing, sneezing, or even speaking to or breathing on other people. In this form, plague can easily wipe out villages in days, towns in weeks, and cities over the course of a few months. No matter how it is spread, the organism of plague, *Yersinia pestis*, multiplies in the victim's bloodstream, poisoning the blood and thus causing death.

After the Plague of Justinian, bubonic plague became endemic—that is, a small number of cases occurred constantly—throughout the world. And there was one worldwide epidemic. This was the so-called Black Death that ravaged Europe (1346–61), reducing the population in some areas by two-thirds and even three-fourths. Plagues recurred in Europe during the next three centuries. A virulent outbreak in London (1664–65) claimed more than 70,000 of the city's 460,000 inhabitants. By July 1665, 2,500 people were dying per week, and by the epidemic's peak in mid-September, more than 7,000 deaths were recorded each week.

Since then, the disease has disappeared from much of the world. No one is quite sure why, although medical historian Frederic Cartwright offers an intriguing explanation in *Disease and History*. He points out that the most common carrier of bubonic plague is the black rat, an animal that lives very close to humans, especially in cramped areas with large human populations and little or no sanitation—conditions that existed throughout the world's urban centers until the 17th century. It was only then that European cities devised sanitation systems, clearing streets of the raw sewage that supplied food for the black rats. In addition, the rodents' chief enemy, the brown (field) rat, began to prey on the black rats and reduced their population.

THEORIES

When the Justinian epidemic occurred, Christianity was the official religion of the Roman Empire, and Christians relied primarily on prayer to cure disease. Indeed, most of the miracles ascribed to Jesus have to do with healing. Bubonic plague was one scourge that Christ was said to be able to cure.

Another was leprosy, known today in medical terms as Hansen's disease, after the Norwegian physician Gerhard Hansen (1841–1912), who first described the microorganism that causes it. Leprosy occurs when *Mycobacterium leprae* invades a patient's skin and nerves. Lumps cover the entire body, and sufferers undergo nerve damage so severe they cannot feel pain. Hence they become susceptible to all sorts of injuries, including cuts, burns, and animal bites. Many lepers lose fingers and toes.

A passage from the New Testament, Mark 1:40–42, describes an encounter between Jesus and a leper:

A medieval painting of a leper seeking a priest's aid. Leprosy, now known as Hansen's disease, is caused by a bacterium that invades the skin and nerves. It usually strikes in warm, damp climates.

> And there came a leper to him, beseeching him, and kneeling down to him, and saying unto him, If thou wilt, thou canst make me clean.
>
> And Jesus, moved with compassion, put forth his hand, and touched him, and saith unto him, I will, be thou clean.
>
> And, as soon as he had spoken, immediately the leprosy departed from him, and he was cleansed.

Cartwright argues that in the Gospel of Saint Mark, as well as in other ancient and medieval writings about disease, leprosy was possibly a generic term used to describe the often horrible skin eruptions caused by many infections, including bubonic plague, smallpox, measles, and syphilis.

By the Middle Ages, European scientists understood that diseases struck without any supernatural assistance. But scientists did not yet realize that disease was spread by unsanitary living conditions. Christian physicians—more faith healers than doctors—continued to hope for supernatural intervention. They devised remedies, but they usually consisted of ineffective ingredients.

In the 17th century, practical medical knowledge began to grow. The English scientist William Harvey (1578–1657) rejected the traditional belief that the blood was made up of "spirits" and "humors" (body fluids) and that "bad" humors caused disease. Harvey theorized that blood circulates through the heart to the lungs, through the arteries, and ultimately back to the heart via the veins. These insights and those of others who followed Harvey set the stage for the understanding of how diseases invade the body and how they might be stopped.

Scientists applied their discoveries to another disease that had claimed many European lives from the Middle Ages to the 17th century: tuberculosis (TB). It is a contagious respiratory ailment that may damage many of the body's organs, most often the lungs. Tuberculosis is spread when an infected person coughs up sputum, which is made up of the mucus produced by cells lining the bronchial tree and of old cells shed from this lining. The bloodstream often carries the disease to the bones, the brain, and the urinary tract.

Anthropologists have found possible traces of TB in the bones of prehistoric people of the Neolithic period (roughly between 4000 and 2000 b.c.). It is also described in the medical writings of ancient China and early Islam. In the Middle Ages, TB was so widespread that it was often referred to as the white plague. It often proved fatal, and those who contracted it were confined to sanatoriums, where they were isolated from other people. Treatment centering on drugs and rest was devised in the early 20th

A ferry converted to a floating hospital for tuberculosis patients, 1912. Isolating the stricken was common before World War II, as they spread the TB bacterium by coughing.

century, after Robert Koch (1843–1910), a German physician and pioneer bacteriologist, isolated the infectious agent of tuberculosis, *Mycobacterium tuberculosis*, in 1882.

An equally ancient disease is smallpox, which is described in medical writings from ancient China, India, and Africa. It is caused by a virus of the *Poxviridae*, or poxvirus family, and is also known as *Variola major*. Smallpox is highly contagious.

Before the 17th century, smallpox was not of much concern in Europe. It was a relatively mild disease and seldom fatal. Occasional epidemics occurred, including the one that killed Mary II, queen of England, in 1694. But in the early 18th century, smallpox became more virulent and emerged as the largest killer of children throughout Europe. Swedish physician Rosen von Rosenstein stated that the disease annually killed 1 in 10 Swedish infants in their first year. It was widespread in 18th-century England and reached the colonies in North America. So deadly was smallpox that the British used it as a form of biological warfare by giving blankets infected with the disease to American Indians.

VACCINATION

In 1796, Edward Jenner (1749–1823), an English physician in the dairy-farming area of Gloucestershire, administered the first smallpox vaccination. It was also the first vaccination used against any disease. Jenner created his vaccination by taking the pus from a cowpox lesion on the hand of a young woman and rubbing it into the open scratch of a young boy. A few weeks later, Jenner "inoculated" the boy with smallpox. The boy did not become ill.

Cowpox, a variation of smallpox, is lethal to animals but generally harmless to humans, although humans do develop some lesions. For centuries, medical folklore had held that infection with cowpox would immunize someone against smallpox. Jenner's vaccination experiments with "humanized cowpox" replaced the older, dangerous technique of "variolation," that is, deliberately infecting a person with a mild smallpox infection by taking pus from a smallpox lesion. Variolation usually led to only mild cases of smallpox in those who were infected, but it made them contagious and capable of passing the lethal infection on to others.

Jenner devised a method for combating smallpox. However, he did not understand exactly why inoculation worked. That

21

Edward Jenner (1749–1823), a British physician, inoculates a baby with the smallpox virus, inducing a mild infection. Jenner noticed that people who had had cowpox did not get smallpox because their body had built up an immunity through exposure.

knowledge did not come for another century, when sophisticated laboratory research began.

In 1677, Antonie van Leeuwenhoek (1632–1723), a Dutch microscopist, developed the first microscope lens. It enabled scientists to see bacteria for the first time. He also saw organisms such as yeasts, molds, and algae and identified red blood cells within the capillaries (the smallest blood vessels) of the skin. These discoveries added evidence to the theory—as old as Lucretius—that diseases could be caused by particles too small to be seen by conventional means.

It was not until the 19th century, however, that scientists gathered sufficient evidence to propose the theory of contagion—the idea that diseases pass directly from person to person. In the 1840s, Ignaz Semmelweis, an assistant at an obstetrics clinic in Vienna, Austria, tried to prove that the transmission of bacteria from patient to patient by obstetricians and other health-care workers caused puerperal fever, also known as childbed fever—a fatal illness in women who have just given birth.

Semmelweis showed that women who contracted this illness had been cared for by doctors and medical students who, without first washing their hands, entered the pregnancy ward directly after having studied cadavers in the autopsy lab. The connection between lack of hand washing and infection seemed obvious, but most of his colleagues dismissed it as nonsense. Many years passed before the idea was widely accepted.

Joseph Lister (1827–1912) carried the work of Semmelweis a step further. From his position as a professor of surgery in Glasgow, Scotland, Lister began the practice of antisepsis (the cleaning of areas where germs may be) and later asepsis (creating a germ-free environment) to aid in the healing of wounds. Lister's first, crude antiseptic technique was to pour carbolic acid on wounds. Later, he used milder substances. He noticed dramatic improvements in the outcome of his surgery, as far fewer patients died from the gangrene that developed in their open wounds.

In 1906, Lister spoke before the British Association for the Advancement of Science:

> Nothing was formerly more striking in surgical experience than the difference in the behavior of injuries according to whether the skin was implicated or not. Thus, if the bones of the leg were broken and the skin remained intact, the surgeon applied the necessary apparatus without any other anxiety than that of maintaining a good position of the fragments, although internal injury to bones and soft part might be severe. If, on the other hand, a wound of the skin

Doctors extract some cowpox-infected tissue from a cow. The vaccine for cowpox was the first to be made from the virus itself, a method, devised by Edward Jenner, that is now standard.

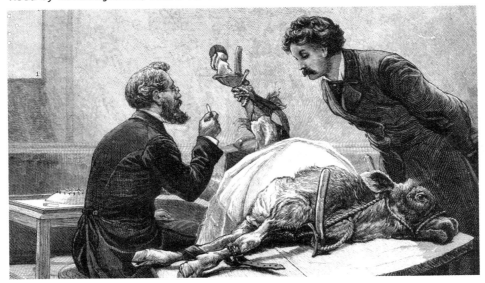

was present communicating with the broken bones, although the damage might be in other respects comparatively slight, the compound fracture, as it was termed, was one of the most dangerous accidents that could happen.

. . . If the wound could be treated with some substance, which without doing too serious mischief to the human tissues would kill the microbes also contained in it and prevent the future access of others in the living state, putrefication [infection] might be prevented.

Lister began as a surgeon. Another great scientist, Louis Pasteur (1822–1895), began as a chemist. He had studied problems of fermentation, trying to find the basic organisms that caused fermentation of acidic substances and, by extension, spoilage of dairy products. Pasteur produced vaccines against anthrax (a disease of farm animals) and rabies, among others. He discovered that bacteria could be killed—usually by heating them to a very high temperature—but would still retain their ability to act as an *antigen*, a substance that stimulates an immune response. Thus, when injected into a patient, dead bacteria activated the body's immune system without triggering the disease.

One day, Pasteur's assistants told him they had left cultures of chicken-cholera microbes in the drying oven for an entire night, thus destroying their capacity to infect chickens. Pasteur then conducted a careful set of experiments. They disclosed that the chicken vaccinated with the cooked chicken-cholera bacteria was permanently immune to chicken cholera.

Pasteur's contemporary Robert Koch, a professor of medicine in Berlin, proved that anthrax was caused by a bacterium. He discovered this by growing the bacteria in his laboratory in a number of different liquid mediums. Each new generation of the bacteria showed the same level of virulence (potential for infection) as the preceding one. Thus, Koch established that diseases do not simply die out. Pasteur seized on this proof, added it to his knowledge that specific bacteria caused each particular disease, and set out to isolate other microbes. He eventually found the microbes that cause puerperal fever.

Koch's and Pasteur's breakthroughs did not immediately lead to wide-scale inoculation against infectious diseases. Well into the 20th century, many infectious diseases, including TB, still

Joseph Lister (1827–1912), British surgeon and scientist. His advances in antiseptic surgery stemmed from the knowledge that disease-causing bacteria are too small to be visible to the naked eye.

raged out of control. Indeed, in 1918 alone, 118,000 Americans died of TB, according to the National Center for Health Statistics. Leprosy also continued into modern times. In the late 19th century, leper colonies sprang up all over the world. They were meant not only to help prevent the spread of the disease, but also to provide an isolated community for the horribly disfigured victims of the disease.

After World War II, massive vaccination programs in the industrial world had begun to stem the tide of many epidemic diseases—most notably smallpox and the childhood illnesses of measles, mumps, and rubella (German measles). The discovery of antibacterial drugs, such as penicillin in 1941, paved the way for the greatest gains in public-health efforts to combat infectious diseases. There are literally hundreds of antibacterial drugs today, and they can be used to treat almost every bacterial infection.

Some diseases, however, remain unexplained. And some that are rare in the developed parts of the world, leprosy for instance, are still widespread in Third World countries. Even when cures or preventive measures exist for certain diseases, they still ravage some places because of unsanitary water, food, and housing; because of overcrowding and malnutrition; or because impoverished peoples cannot afford the vaccinations.

VIRUSES: TODAY'S INFECTIOUS ENEMIES

In the 1890s, Pierre-Paul-Emile Roux, a French bacteriologist, discovered the existence of organisms smaller than bacteria: viruses. They could not be identified, though, until the 1930s, when

the electron microscope was invented. Prior to that, viruses could only be studied indirectly through the symptoms of the diseases they were believed to have produced.

Viral diseases devastated populations throughout the world into the middle of the 20th century. The influenza epidemic of 1917–1919, caused by the influenza virus, claimed thousands of lives worldwide. New strains of influenza—commonly called the flu—caused periodic outbreaks of epidemic proportion even in the 1980s, and will undoubtedly recur in the future.

AIDS, which some have called the Black Death of the 1980s, is a fatal viral illness that in the United States afflicts primarily homosexual and bisexual men, users of intravenous drugs, individuals with hemophilia and other recipients of blood products, and the heterosexual sex partners of people in these high-risk groups. Children of infected individuals can acquire the disease before or during birth, although evidence of the disease often does not appear for a number of months after birth.

As of January 1989, about 85,000 people in America had been diagnosed as having AIDS, and about 48,000 of them had died. Nearly all those with the virus are expected to die within three to five years of being diagnosed, usually from one of a number of other infections that complicate AIDS. Surgeon General C. Everett Koop estimated that more than 1 million Americans had been infected with the AIDS virus, known medically as the human immunodeficiency virus (HIV).

AIDS and other viral illnesses represent the challenge for infectious-disease specialists in the years to come.

•   •   •   •

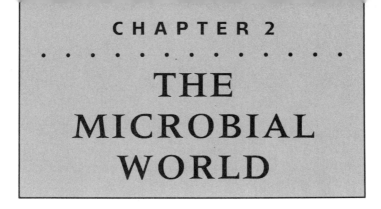

CHAPTER 2

THE MICROBIAL WORLD

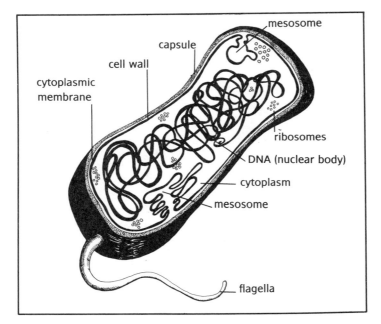

Bacterial cell, also called prokaryote.

Any discussion of infectious diseases must begin with an explanation of how bacteria, viruses, and other microorganisms attack the human body and, in turn, of how the human body defends itself. Bacteria—also called prokaryotes—belong to the biological kingdom known as the Protista, or Monera. Simple organisms usually composed of a single cell, prokaryotes have no distinct nucleus—the area where genetic material is stored. The basic components of prokaryotic cells include the following.

Cytoplasmic membrane (cell membrane): An envelope that keeps some components inside the cell and allows the exchange of certain nutrients and other components across it. The membrane is made up of molecules of protein and of phospholipid, a type of fat.

Mesosome: A section of the cell membrane pushed into the cytoplasm. Its function is not well understood, but it seems to help in the process whereby genetic material is copied, enabling one cell to divide into two.

Cell wall: A protective coating, composed of sugar and protein molecules, that makes the outside of the cell rigid.

Model of a DNA molecule. In 1956, American James Watson and Englishman Francis Crick discovered the structure of this key molecule.

Capsule: Another protective coating found in some bacteria. It appears outside the cell wall and is usually made up of sugar molecules. It possibly makes bacteria more resistant to attacks from the immune system.

Cytoplasm: The fluid filling the cell membrane, where ribosomes and the nuclear body are located.

Nuclear body: The area of the cell where the genetic material is stored. In the case of bacteria, this genetic material is deoxyribonucleic acid (DNA), which is composed of paired nitrogenous bases that form a code used by all bacterial, plant, and animal cells to store information. These chains of information, twisted around each other to form a molecule of DNA, enable the cell to survive and reproduce. In bacteria, the chain becomes a circle that then twists around itself in a genetically determined pattern. The code is then translated into proteins by the ribosomes that float in the cytoplasm.

Ribosomes: Decoding structures, located in the cytoplasm, that translate DNA into proteins using an intermediary called ribonucleic acid (RNA), which is nearly identical to DNA except that it comes in single strands and contains the nitrogenous base uracil instead of thymine. (Some viruses have no DNA and rely on RNA as their only source of genetic information.)

BACTERIA AND INFECTIONS

Most bacteria cause infection by entering the body through the respiratory tract (breathing), gastrointestinal tract (eating, digesting, and depositing solid waste), urinary tract (disposing of liquid wastes), genital tract (reproduction), or through scrapes in the skin. Some can be transmitted through coughing or sneezing. They can also be transmitted into the skin or directly into the bloodstream by the bite of an infected animal or insect.

In many bacteria, built-in components protect them from the host's defense mechanisms. Some bacteria invade, multiply, and then produce a toxin (poison) that is responsible for the actual signs and symptoms of the illness in the host, which may include fever, destruction of body tissues, paralysis, muscle spasms, or severe vomiting and diarrhea. Other bacteria produce substances that dissolve tissue components in the host and allow the bacteria to spread through the tissues toward target organs with or without passage into the bloodstream.

Not all bacteria are harmful. Many microorganisms—known as normal flora—live on the skin and in the respiratory, gastrointestinal, and genitourinary systems without causing infection. A few normal flora even play important roles in maintaining body function. For instance, some bacteria in the gastrointestinal tract are responsible for the formation of vitamin K, an important blood-clotting factor. But if the surface of the skin is disturbed by a cut or a scrape, normal skin flora can enter the wound and multiply, causing an infection.

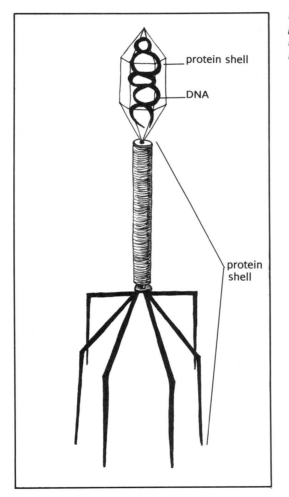

Diagram of a bacteriophage, a type of virus. It is present in sewage and in body products.

VIRUSES

Viruses are the smallest infectious agents that scientists have yet identified. The diameter of a virus measures from 0.01 to 0.3 micrometers (a micrometer is one-millionth of a meter), as opposed to the 0.2 to 2.0 micrometers that the diameter of a bacterium measures. Unlike bacteria, whose genetic material is composed exclusively of DNA, viruses contain either DNA or RNA, but never both. Indeed, viruses can be classified by the type of genetic material they possess—DNA or RNA, single strand or double strand. Also unlike bacteria, viruses cannot reproduce on their own. A virus must enter a living cell, such as a human or animal cell; incorporate its genome (the DNA or RNA portion of the virus) into the host cell's genetic material; and then force these cells to make viral components.

Whether the virus contains DNA or RNA, all viruses have some basic structural components in common. These include the following.

Core: The viral genome.

Capsid: The protein capsule that encases the genetic material. Viruses can be classified according to the capsid's shape.

Nucleocapsid: The combination of core and capsid envelope.

In other words, viruses reproduce by entering a cell and incorporating their material into the genetic material of that host cell. In cells other than bacteria, the host's gene is located in the area of the cell called the nucleus, a portion of the cell surrounded by its own membrane. Once the viral genome has been copied, it is translated into the proteins needed for the capsid. The capsid surrounds the copy of its gene and then breaks through the nucleus into the cytoplasm, taking a piece of the nuclear membrane with it. This piece of host nuclear membrane is known as the envelope. The envelope's evident purpose is to protect the new viral particle from enzymes (a kind of protein) located in the host cytoplasm, which could destroy it.

VIRUSES AND INFECTIONS

Viruses, like bacteria, can cause infections by entering the body through scrapes in the skin or through the respiratory, gastrointestinal, or genitourinary tracts. They then invade the cells of one or more organs (including the skin), multiply, escape from their original site into the blood, and infect other organs where they can reproduce again.

Viral particles can be transmitted from person to person through coughing or sneezing and through sexual contact. They can also be transmitted by the bite of an infected animal or insect.

THE IMMUNE RESPONSE

Once a bacteria or virus invades the body, the body has several ways of fighting off infection. The first line of defense is the skin, as well as the linings of the mouth, nose, and stomach. The linings of the mouth and nose (mucous membranes) produce enzymes that dissolve microorganisms along with mucus that snares the infectious particles and pushes them away. The stomach, for its part, forms acid that can kill most invading microorganisms.

The initial response the body makes to any type of injury, whether or not infection results, is called inflammation. There are four classic signs of inflammation, as described in the 1st century A.D. by Cornelius Celsus, a Roman scholar. They are *rubor* (redness), *tumor* (swelling), *calor* (warmth), and *dolor* (pain).

These signs appear, for example, after a skin cut. First, in the area of the cut, small blood vessels dilate. This makes the skin red and warm and causes blood to flow into the affected area, bringing the blood components that help repair the injury and fight against possible infection. Plasma, the clear fluid part of the blood, leaks into the area, which causes swelling. At the same time, the blood begins to clot. Pain arises from injury done to nerve fibers in the skin and also from the pressure caused by swelling.

Blood components that actively defend the body after an invasion by bacteria or viruses are white blood cells (WBCs). There are various types of WBCs—lymphocytes, polymorphonuclear cells, and macrophages—that inactivate, "eat," or dissolve invading microorganisms. The damaged tissue, microorganisms, and WBCs then combine to form pus, a yellowish-white fluid. For many centuries—up through the Middle Ages, in fact—pus was thought to be a positive part of the healing process. Today, we know that pus signals the onset of infection, which must be treated.

The Roman medical writer Aulus Cornelius Celsus (25 B.C.—A.D. 50) described inflammation from infection, listing its symptoms as redness, swelling, warmth, and pain.

The body usually responds to the presence of an antigen—that is, to bacteria, viruses, and any other particle that activates the body's immune system—by forming a type of protein called an immunoglobulin, or antibody. There are five basic types of immunoglobulins: IgG, IgM, IgA, IgD, and IgE (the last letter of each type designates a chemical component), but only the first three are important in the body's defense against antigens.

IgA is present in saliva, in tears, and in the mucus secreted by the respiratory, gastrointestinal, urinary, and genital tracts. It is thus part of the first line of defense against invading microorganisms. When an antigen eludes this initial defense and penetrates either body tissues or the bloodstream or both, lymphocytes—the WBCs responsible for creating antibodies—

respond by producing IgM and IgG. These antibodies bind to the surface of the bacterium or virus or to the toxin that a bacterium may produce. In some instances, an antigen will be inactivated or neutralized if an antibody binds to it. In other instances, the antibody actually breaks down or dissolves the antigen. In still other cases, the antibody coats the antigen and makes it available for destruction by polymorphonuclear cells and macrophages.

One of the important features of lymphocytes is called immunologic memory, which works in the following way: The first time the body is exposed to an antigen—for instance, the varicella virus (chicken pox)—lymphocytes manufacture a lot of IgM and some IgG, which help fight the infection. Some of the lymphocytes "remember" the antigen, and if the body is exposed to chicken pox a second time, a lot of IgG and a little IgM are formed right away, preventing the development of a rash and other symptoms of chicken pox.

This 1893 engraving shows an early effort at large-scale immunization of the public, such as for homeless lodgers. Despite scientific progress in combating disease, the conditions that serve as breeding grounds for communicable diseases have not been wiped out.

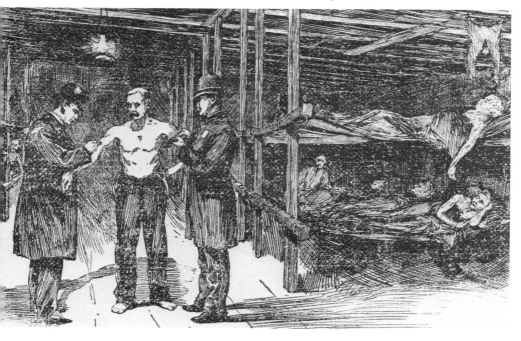

IMMUNIZATIONS

Immunologic memory is critical to the success of immunizations, including the series of "baby shots" most children in the United States and in many other countries receive in childhood and the vaccinations one may receive before traveling to a foreign country. The goal of any vaccination is for the body to produce lymphocytes with a memory of the disease, so that once someone is exposed to the actual disease, IgG and IgM will form quickly, and the body will manage to fight off the invader.

There are two types of immunity, active and passive. In active immunization, the body is exposed to an antigen and, ideally, develops the appropriate antibody response. In passive immunization, physicians take antibodies from different people, pool them, and then give them to someone who has been exposed to an antigen but cannot produce a rapid response or any response at all.

In recent times, many types of immunizations have been developed. Most are live or killed bacteria or viruses. A live vaccine causes a mild version of the disease it is designed to protect against—usually a slight fever and rash—and leaves the body with a "memory" of the disease. Other immunizations include partly inactivated toxins called toxoids. The toxoid is potent enough to induce an immune response but not potent enough to cause disease. Still other types are components of the outer coatings of the microorganism. Like the toxoid, these components can induce an immune response. Since the advent of genetic engineering in the 1960s, scientists have sought to create vaccines for viruses.

ANTIMICROBIAL AGENTS

There are many infections that the immune system cannot destroy without help from antibiotics and antiviral drugs. Since penicillin was discovered in 1941, thousands of drugs to treat infectious diseases have been produced. They mainly treat bacterial infections because viral infections usually require no medication. Sometimes, however, a viral infection may be so severe that medications are used, particularly to aid people with deficient immune systems.

Most antibiotics work by inhibiting the production of some part of the bacterial cell, either molecules of the cell wall, portions of the genome, or other necessary proteins. Antiviral agents generally inhibit replication of the viral genome. This keeps the microorganism from multiplying and brings the infection under control.

•   •   •   •

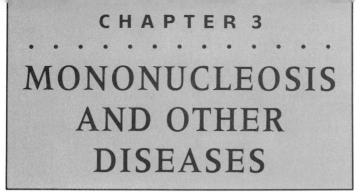

CHAPTER 3
· · · · · · · · · · · · ·
MONONUCLEOSIS AND OTHER DISEASES

Infectious mononucleosis, known as "mono," or "the kissing disease," is a debilitating but not life-threatening disease caused by the Epstein-Barr virus (EBV). Mono typically afflicts adolescents and college students, although its victims also include children, particularly in Third World countries.

The term *kissing disease* is not as silly as it seems: EBV is passed from person to person via saliva, usually by kissing or by sharing a glass, silverware, or a toothbrush. Because the incubation period (the interval of time that elapses from the moment one is first exposed to a disease until the first symptoms appear) lasts one to two months, it can be difficult to pinpoint the source of the infection.

The first signs of mononucleosis are usually fatigue, headache, and malaise—a general feeling of ill health. Soon the victim develops nausea, abdominal pain, fever, and a sore throat. Because the sore throat can be severe, and because the patient's tonsils may enlarge and be covered with pus, the disease is occasionally mistaken for strep throat. Someone with mono typically suffers swollen lymph nodes, particularly in the neck. Other symptoms include a tender and enlarged spleen and liver.

Inflammation of the liver amounts to a mild form of hepatitis. The spleen becomes swollen and may actually rupture, a condition that can be caused by any sort of trauma, from a soft bump on the abdomen to a football tackle. For this reason, doctors often discourage patients from athletic activity during the first month or so after they have been diagnosed, when the danger of a rupture is greatest. In some cases, however, the spleen ruptures for no apparent reason. In any case, if a ruptured spleen is not detected and treated quickly, it can cause death from internal bleeding.

In order to confirm a diagnosis of mono, doctors must perform blood tests. One reliable test is the complete blood count (CBC), which measures the number of red and white blood cells. Mononucleosis raises the total white blood cell (WBC) count and causes an increase in the percentage of blood cells made up by lymphocytes. Under microscopic examination, many of these lymphocytes look abnormal; they are referred to as "atypical" lymphocytes.

People infected with the EBV may produce a host of other, less specific, antibodies known as heterophile antibodies. A doctor may call for a lab procedure called a monospot, or heterophile, antibody test, in which a sample of the patient's blood is mixed with red blood cells from a sheep or horse. If the red blood cells in the test clump together, the patient has tested positive. If he or she also exhibits clinical symptoms, all uncertainty is erased: The patient has mono.

These blood tests help differentiate mono from the host of other illnesses—including hepatitis—that have similar symptoms. Cultures and blood tests will also rule out strep throat. In some instances, it may even be necessary to investigate a person's

The British physician William Harvey (1578– 1657) discovered that blood circulates through- out the body in a closed system.

bone marrow to rule out leukemia, a cancer of the white blood cells, the symptoms of which also resemble those associated with mono.

Infectious mononucleosis can lead to a variety of complications, some mild, others severe. The tonsils can become so enlarged that they block the airway and make breathing difficult. Mono can also be complicated by pneumonia and myocarditis, an inflammation of the heart muscle. Other complications range from a stiff neck, dizziness, and ataxia (difficulty walking in a straight line) to meningitis or encephalitis, inflammations of the covering of the brain and spinal cord or of the brain tissue itself. These illnesses can cause the patient to suffer seizures or convulsions and in severe cases can result in death.

An unusual form of paralysis, resulting from the Guillain-Barré syndrome, has been associated with mono. This condition, which seems to occur spontaneously, causes temporary paralysis of some or all of the muscles in the patient's body. The condition usually reverses itself, but many people are weakened for a long time—weeks or even months. As yet, no treatment exists.

A few other diseases have been associated with EBV. Two forms of cancer—Burkitt's lymphoma and nasopharyngeal carcinoma—have been linked to EBV. The EBV-associated Burkitt's lymphoma is a tumor of the jaw found most often in African children. Nasopharyngeal carcinoma, a cancer of the nose and throat, is most common in Chinese and Eskimo adults.

Although most cases of infectious mono last from a few weeks to a few months, there is some evidence that there is a form of the disease, known as chronic mono, or chronic EBV syndrome, that can last for many months or even years. People who suffer from chronic mono may struggle in school or at work because they are so ill so often.

Not all those who exhibit lingering symptoms have large numbers of antibodies circulating in their blood. Thus, physicians are divided about whether chronic EBV syndrome exists as a definable and treatable disease. Some physicians suspect that patients who complain of continual fatigue and other mono-related symptoms may have a psychosomatic illness, that is, physical symptoms with a psychological rather than a physical cause.

Infectious mono is treated like other viral infections. No specific medication can do the trick; the immune system must clear the infection itself. Patients usually can speed their recovery, however, by resting, drinking lots of fluids, and keeping their fever in check. If swollen tonsils threaten a person's ability to breathe, steroids (medications that can reduce inflammation) may help lessen swelling.

CHILDHOOD DISEASES

Before routine immunization became available, chicken pox, measles, mumps, and rubella were among the diseases most commonly contracted by American children. These illnesses were so widespread that many mothers intentionally exposed their school-age children to infected children in order to "get the illness over with." Most children developed mild infections that cleared up by themselves, but some patients—children and adults—died from these diseases or were left with various disabilities, including, in the most severe cases, brain damage. Because infection leads to immunity, these illnesses strike only once.

Now that the measles-mumps-rubella (MMR) vaccine is given to nearly all children at the age of 15 months, these 3 illnesses no longer strike in epidemic numbers. There are occasional outbreaks, however, such as the measles epidemics reported at many American colleges in the mid-1980s. Most of the victims had been inoculated prior to 1967, when the measles component in the vaccine was incapable of providing lasting immunity.

Chicken pox is still a very common infection among children and adults. A vaccine against chicken pox was developed in the 1980s, but as of 1989, it was available only to people with a serious disease, such as cancer, or to people with abnormal immune systems. Similarly, immunoglobulins are available for all these infections but are given only to people with severe illnesses or immune deficiencies and who are exposed to others with chicken pox, measles, mumps, or rubella.

Chicken Pox

Chicken pox, or varicella, is caused by the herpesvirus varicella-zoster. It usually strikes between January and May. It is spread by coughing or by contact with the fluid inside the lesions, such as touching an open wound on an infected person. The incubation period lasts 10 days to 3 weeks. Chicken pox is most prevalent in children under 10, but anyone can get it. The first symptom of chicken pox is a general feeling of discomfort that last about 24 hours and is accompanied by a slight fever. Next comes a rash, characterized by small red papules (bumps) that cause itching and flatten into the shape of a teardrop. In the middle of the bumps, a tiny vesicle (blister) develops, initially filled with clear fluid. After about 24 hours, the fluid becomes cloudy. Then the vesicle breaks open, and a scab forms. The fluid within the vesicle contains infectious material. New lesions continue to crop up for three or four days.

The patient's temperature can climb to 103 or even to 105 degrees Fahrenheit as the rash spreads. Generally, the lesions appear first on the chest, abdomen, and back, then on the face and scalp, and then on the arms and legs. They can occur anywhere, including inside the mouth, nose, ears, and the genitourinary tract. Some patients have only a few lesions; others develop hundreds.

Complications of chicken pox include superinfections—simultaneous infections of the lesions by bacteria from the skin—

(continued on page 45)

Three Pioneers

Dr. Jonas Salk, who developed the first polio vaccine.

Until the mid-20th century, one of the most devastating of all infectious diseases, especially for young people, was poliomyelitis, also known as infantile paralysis. This ailment, spread through contact with infected persons, is carried by a virus that enters the victim's mouth and then passes into the bloodstream. In most cases, only a few symptoms appear and no serious illness occurs. But if the virus penetrates the central nervous system, lesions can form on the brain and spinal cord, and the victim suffers paralysis or even death.

For centuries, polio claimed thousands of victims annually. Then, around 1910, Sister Elizabeth Kenny, an Australian nurse, devised a unique treatment. (She was not a nun; a head nurse in British countries then was called "sister.") First she dispensed with the patient's casts and splints. Then she soaked a woolen cloth in hot water and wrapped it around the patient's stricken legs and arms. Next, she lightly exercised the limbs, helping to restimulate them. This therapy did not always work. Indeed, only a few patients, most of them children, fully recovered. But Sister Kenny's treatment, though not a cure, gave hope to those routinely written off by medical experts.

The experts were not persuaded by her technique, however. When the Australian nurse came to the United States in 1940 and established the Elizabeth Kenny Institute, in Minneapolis, Minnesota, some researchers objected that her method was not medically sound and should not be taught to others. They changed their minds when they saw the results Sister Kenny achieved. Soon her treatment became standard.

The next major breakthrough came in 1953, when Dr. Jonas Edward Salk, a physician and microbiologist born and educated in New York City, developed the first polio vaccine. He made it by cultivating three strains of the virus in monkey tissue, which he stored for a week and then treated with formaldehyde, a colorless gas that killed the virus. The dead virus became a vaccine that immunized people against the disease after three or four injections. By 1955, the Salk vaccine had been administered widely in the United States and with great success. It was not flawless, however. One problem was that the vaccine guarded only against paralysis and not against infection. Another was that the immunization wore off soon.

These shortcomings were remedied by the third polio pioneer, Albert Bruce Sabin, a native of Poland who emigrated to the United States in 1921 and received his education in New York City. His research on infectious diseases led to the development, in 1959, of a new polio vaccine composed of a live, rather than dead, virus. Sabin's vaccine, which is taken orally rather than by injection, prevents both infection and paralysis and immunizes the patient for a longer period of time than the dead-virus vaccine. In 1961, Sabin's vaccine was ready for use throughout the United States, and one of the most feared infectious diseases had ceased to be a major threat.

Chicago, 1956. Polio shots became widely available after Dr. Bruce Sabin developed a vaccine more effective than the Salk vaccine. By the early 1960s, poliomyelitis had been largely eradicated.

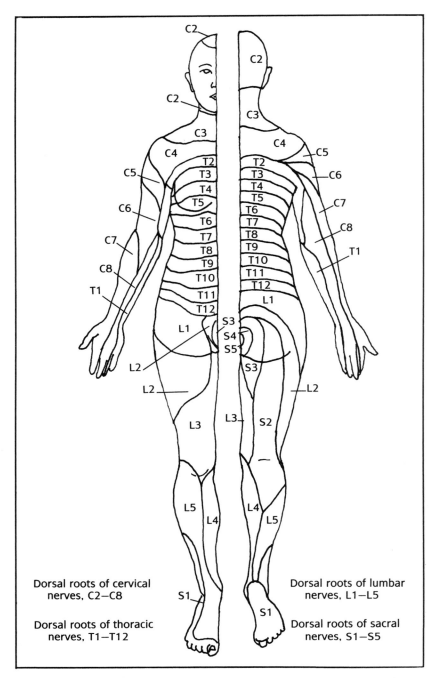

Diagram of dermatomes, the series of skin segments where feeling is supplied by the branches of individual nerve roots. The blisters of some diseases, including shingles, are limited to one dermatome.

(continued from page 41)

and also pneumonia, infections of the heart, kidneys, liver, joints, and brain (encephalitis). The most common complication, by far, is superinfection. In general, only adults infected with chicken pox or children with abnormal immune systems need worry about the infection spreading to organs other than the skin. Should the infection spread, however, the damage can be severe.

Treatments for chicken pox focus on the itching and fever. Two antiviral drugs, adenine arabinoside and acyclovir, often prove useful in severe cases, particularly if the patient has a faulty immune system. Antibiotics are useful only against bacterial superinfections of the skin and other organs.

Once the chicken pox infection has cleared, some viral particles enter the nervous system and travel to the nerve roots along the spinal cord. These particles exist in a dormant, or noninfectious, state unless some sort of stress or illness weakens the immune system. If this happens, an outbreak of herpes zoster, or shingles, can occur. It is an extremely painful ailment that causes blisters to appear on the skin. These resemble chicken pox blisters but are limited to a specific area of skin, called a dermatome, whose feeling is supplied by the branches of individual nerve roots. When herpes zoster is awakened from its dormant state, it generally strikes a single dermatome, often on the chest, abdomen, buttock, or face. If the affected dermatome involves the eye, the patient's vision can be impaired. The older the patient, the more painful the disorder—it rarely causes pain in children but can be excruciating for elderly people. Treatment of herpes zoster is similar to that of chicken pox, with respect to treatment of pain and the use of antiviral agents adenine arabinoside and acyclovir.

Measles

Measles (rubeola) is caused by morbillivirus, a member of the paramyxovirus family. It is transmitted from person to person by respiratory secretions and produces an illness characterized by fever, cough, runny nose, conjunctivitis (inflammation of the white part of the eyes), and a rash.

Measles first strikes the respiratory system, which can be affected for up to 10 days. Two days before the rash begins, Koplik's spots (named for Henry Koplik, 1858–1927, a New York physician who first noticed them) appear inside the mouth. They are blue-white vesicles on a red base. As the rash appears, the spots fade. The rash begins with slightly itchy, pale-red macules (flat lesions) behind the ears and around the edges of the face. This rash spreads to the face, neck, trunk and then to the arms and legs. The macules become slightly raised and bumpy. As the rash spreads down the body, the oldest lesions—those on the face and neck—merge, forming large red areas. Bleeding often occurs within these lesions.

The incubation period for measles is normally two weeks. The respiratory symptoms may begin only a few days after exposure, and the rash may appear two weeks after exposure. Unlike chicken pox, which appears every year in the United States, measles outbreaks generally happen every two to three years.

Complications include middle-ear infection, pneumonia, and encephalitis. A severe type of encephalitis, subacute sclerosing panencephalitis, can result in severe brain damage.

There is no specific treatment for measles. Control of fever and other symptoms is helpful.

Mumps

Mumps—epidemic parotitis—is caused by the mumps virus, another paramyxovirus. It produces inflammation of the parotid glands, which are saliva-producing glands located below the ear. Sometimes mumps also inflames salivary glands under the tongue and under the jaw. Only about one-third to one-half of

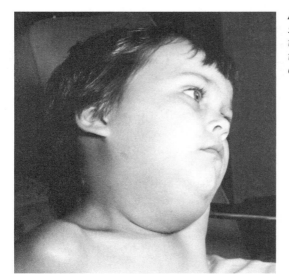

A child with mumps. The swelling of glands in the throat is characteristic of the infection, which is caused by a virus.

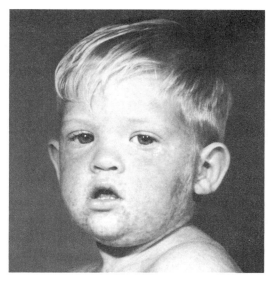

A child with rubella, or German measles. Highly contagious because it is spread by respiratory secretions, this viral infection usually strikes in grade school. It is a milder disease than measles.

all those infected with the mumps virus will actually show symptoms of the disease. The ailment begins with fever, malaise, and pain in the neck and head. Next comes painful swelling of the parotid glands, though sometimes only one side of the face is affected. Eating anything sour during this time can produce severe pain because the inflamed parotid glands must produce more saliva. Occasionally, a red rash appears on the chest, abdomen, and back.

Mumps occurs all year round but strikes most commonly in late winter and early spring. It is spread by respiratory secretions and possibly also by urine. The contagious period lasts from 1 day before the appearance of swelling until 3 days after, and the incubation period is about 14 to 25 days.

Complications of mumps include infection of the testicles in adolescent and adult males, encephalitis, and infections of the heart, kidneys, joints, and eyes. The testicular infection can result in sterility (inability to reproduce), but this rarely happens. Most often only one testis is affected, and the boy or man remains fertile. Encephalitis from mumps may result in deafness or brain damage.

Rubella

Rubella—German measles or three-day measles—is caused by a togavirus. Although it is a relatively mild virus, it can cause multiple birth defects in unborn children when a pregnant woman becomes infected. Before the MMR vaccine, young mothers were fearful of their preschool and school-age children contracting rubella when the mothers were pregnant with another child. The incubation period usually lasts two to three weeks.

Rubella begins with a brief period of respiratory symptoms, followed by swelling of the lymph nodes behind the ears, skull, and along the back of the neck. A few red spots may appear in the mouth. About 24 hours after the lymph nodes swell, a slightly itchy rash begins on the face and spreads to the trunk. The rash comes and goes over the course of one to three days and may actually disappear from the face before it appears on the trunk. The rash may be accompanied by a slight fever and joint pain. Because the disease is quite mild in most cases, treatment is aimed at those pains and the fever and at respiratory symptoms.

Like chicken pox, measles, and mumps, rubella is transmitted by respiratory secretions. Before the availability of the rubella vaccine, outbreaks occurred every six to nine years. Rubella leads to very few complications. It occasionally causes arthritis or encephalitis, but the most devastating effects of rubella are to unborn children. Pregnant women who have never had rubella or the rubella vaccine and who become infected during the first three months of pregnancy risk giving birth to a child with the congenital rubella syndrome. Birth defects associated with this syndrome include various malformations of the heart, infection of the liver, cataracts, deafness, and mental retardation. These infants may also be infectious to others at the time of their birth.

•   •   •   •

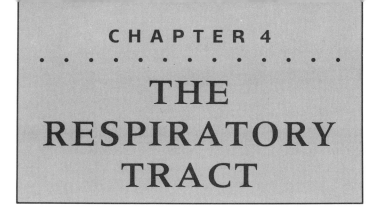

CHAPTER 4

. . . .

THE RESPIRATORY TRACT

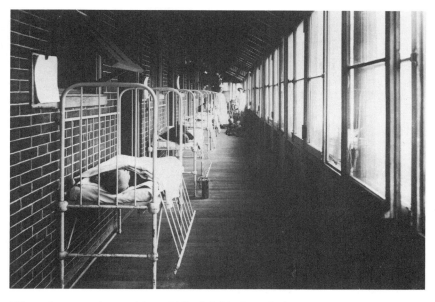

Whooping-cough ward in a Philadelphia hospital, 1910.

During the course of each year, many people catch a cold, a simple name for what is often a complex variety of infections—usually viral—that affect the human respiratory tract. The respiratory tract, which extends from the nose to the lungs, permits us to inhale oxygen and exhale carbon dioxide. The tract is composed of various structures that, when we breathe, filter out large airborne particles. But small particles—bacteria, viruses, and other microorganisms—often slip through and infect us.

Because it is so extensive, the respiratory tract is a common portal

RESPIRATORY TRACT INFECTIONS

for many infectious diseases caused by bacteria, viruses, fungi, and parasites. Most of these ailments are short lived, but a few are difficult to treat and potentially life threatening.

The infections are generally spread by contact with an infected person who coughs or sneezes. Crowded conditions increase the chance that someone will catch one of these infections. Tobacco also heightens the chances of contagion: Children who live among smokers seem more susceptible than other children to respiratory tract infections.

Upper Respiratory Tract Infections

Upper respiratory tract infections (URIs), also known as acute nasopharyngitis or the common cold, are the most common of all infectious illnesses, especially in young children. Research has shown that infants contract a URI once in every one or two exposures to someone with a URI, whereas older children and adults are infected once in every four to five exposures. Even healthy children under the age of five suffer an average of seven to nine URIs a year.

Most URIs are caused by viruses, particularly members of the adenovirus, enterovirus, and parainfluenza virus families, as well as by respiratory syncytial virus and the rhinoviruses. Contrary to popular belief, merely being cold or wet will not cause a cold.

Signs and symptoms of the cold include rhinitis (inflammation of the nasal mucous membrane), rhinorrhea (runny nose), congestion, cough, sneezing, and malaise. They vary in severity from person to person and from cold to cold. Younger children may be more severely affected because they breathe primarily through their nose rather than through their mouth. Possible complications of the common cold include fever, vomiting, and diarrhea, as well as infections of the middle ear and sinuses.

The treatment of URIs is the same as that of most viral illnesses. Controlling fever is helpful. Probably the best therapy is to keep the airways moist by drinking lots of fluids and either using a vaporizer or saltwater nose drops, or both, particularly for infants. Decongestants and cough medicines may help shrink the swelling of the nasal passages, but they will not shorten the length of the illness. Nor can antibiotics cure a viral infection.

Ear Infections

A common complication of URI is otitis media (infection of the middle ear). When the eustachian tube (the tube linking the middle ear to the pharynx) is blocked, generally by inflammation associated with a cold, negative pressure (a vacuum) develops in the middle ear. Fluid then fills the tube and nourishes the invading microorganisms.

The signs and symptoms of acute otitis media are severe ear pain and fever. They result when the body tries to defend itself

(continued on page 54)

The ear. Infections of the external or middle parts are fairly common. The fluid that forms after infection gives nourishment to the invading microorganisms.

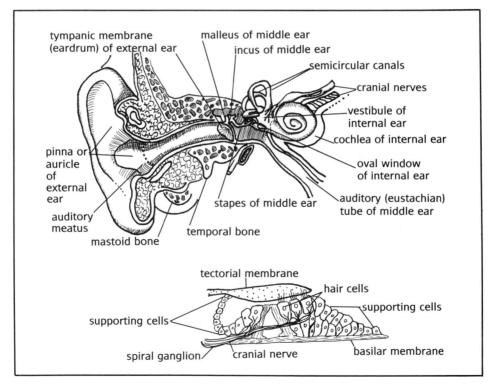

The Respiratory Tract

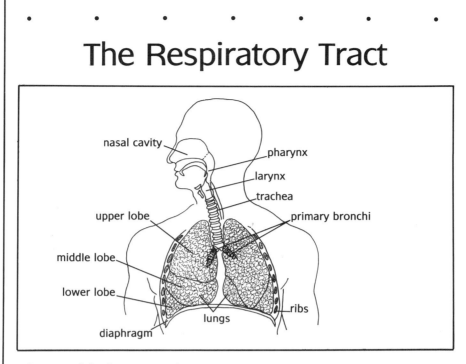

Diagram of the human respiratory system.

The respiratory tract can be divided into two major sections—the conducting portion, which stretches from the nose to the large subdivisions of the bronchial tree (the bronchi together with their branches); and the respiratory portion, which includes the smaller bronchi and the lung tissue. The conducting portion is further divided into the extrathoracic region (outside the chest) and the intrathoracic region (inside the chest).

The nose is not used only for smelling. It also warms inhaled air and filters out many airborne particles by trapping them in mucus produced by cells in the epithelium (lining tissue) of the nasal passages. Hairs that grow from other cells help keep large particles from traveling down the respiratory tract. In addition, immunoglobulin A, secreted by yet another group of cells in the tissue lining the nasal cavity, is useful in preventing many bacterial and viral infections.

The sinuses are air spaces located within the bones of the face and in the area behind the nose. The frontal sinuses are in the forehead, the maxillary sinuses in the cheeks, the ethmoid sinuses above and below the nose, and the sphenoid sinuses behind the ethmoids. Inside the sinuses, the epithelium is made up of hair cells and mucus-producing cells.

The sinuses make the bones of the skull lighter than they would otherwise be and thus more easily supported by the neck muscles and vertebrae. But the primary functions of the sinuses are to warm and moisten air and to act as a second filter for airborne particles. The sinuses drain into the nose through very small passages called ostia. If the ostia become blocked by secretions or inflammation, infections can develop within the sinuses.

The back of the nasal cavity is connected to the pharynx (upper throat) by the nasopharynx, which contains the tonsils as well as the adenoids, which are collections of lymphatic tissue where lymphocytes produce antibodies.

The pharynx is also the site of the oropharynx, a part of both the respiratory and digestive systems. The digestive system continues from the oropharynx into the esophagus, and the respiratory system continues into the larynx (voice box), a hollow tube supported by layers of muscle and some flat pieces of cartilage, including the thyroid cartilage (the Adam's apple.) Another important structure in the larynx is the vocal cords, small, flat semicircles of tissue that separate or meet to produce the different pitches made for speaking and singing.

The sinuses.

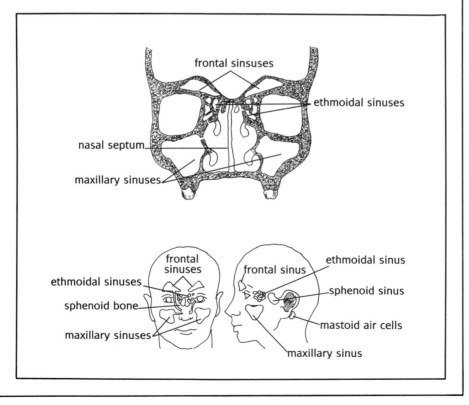

(continued from page 51)

against these microorganisms. Pus forms in the middle ear and the eardrum becomes inflamed, causing pressure to rise in this small and sensitive space. Sometimes the pressure bursts the eardrum, and pus flows into the external ear canal.

The bacteria responsible for most cases of otitis media include *Streptococcus pneumoniae*, *Haemophilus influenzae* (though not type B), and *Branhamella catarrhalis*, all of which can be treated with common oral antibiotics.

Recurrent middle-ear infections can lead to hearing problems. Repeated bouts of inflammation in the middle ear can cause scars to form on the eardrum, and fluid can lodge in the middle ear. These developments hinder the passage of vibrations from the outside world to the inner ear.

Infections of the external ear canal, known as otitis externa, or "swimmer's ear," occur when the protective coating of earwax is damaged and bacteria are allowed to invade the underlying epithelium, the top layer of skin. Most commonly, wax is diminished by constant wetness from swimming (hence the name) and from overly vigorous cleaning of the ear. There is some truth in the humorous axiom, "Never stick anything in your ear smaller than your elbow."

Sinusitis

Sinusitis, another common complication of URI, means inflammation and infection of the sinuses. The ostia (openings) draining the sinuses are very small, and when they become blocked by inflammation of the nasal passages, fluid fills the sinuses. This sets up a perfect environment for infection.

Sinusitis is somewhat more common in older children and adults because the air spaces in the sphenoid sinuses do not fully develop until people reach 3 to 5 years of age and the frontal sinuses do not fully develop before the ages of 6 to 10. People suffering from sinusitis can get headaches caused by pus in the sinuses. The organisms responsible are the same as those that cause otitis media, and the antibiotic treatment is the same.

The infection of sinusitis can extend into those areas bordered by the sinuses—the orbital cavity (the space in the skull where the eyes are located) and the brain. Should they become infected, they must be surgically drained and treated with antibiotics.

The Trachea and Bronchi

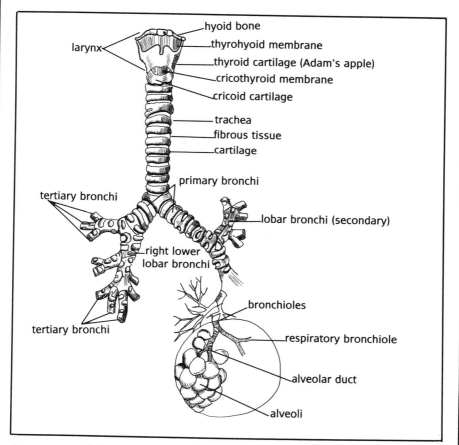

hyoid bone
thyrohyoid membrane
thyroid cartilage (Adam's apple)
cricothyroid membrane
cricoid cartilage

larynx

trachea
fibrous tissue
cartilage

primary bronchi

tertiary bronchi

lobar bronchi (secondary)

right lower
lobar bronchi

bronchioles

respiratory bronchiole

tertiary bronchi

alveolar duct

alveoli

Lower part of the respiratory system, showing the bronchial tree.

The trachea (windpipe), a hollow tube, is situated below the larynx. It is supported by 16 to 20 incomplete rings of cartilage. The trachea divides into two branches, the right and left mainstem bronchi. From this point the bronchial tree divides into smaller and smaller branches within the lungs.

The mainstem bronchi branch off the trachea at slightly different angles, the right mainstem bronchus tilting downward. For this

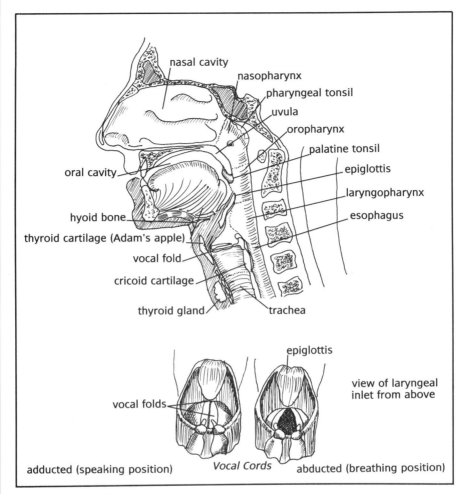

nasal cavity
nasopharynx
pharyngeal tonsil
uvula
oropharynx
palatine tonsil
oral cavity
epiglottis
laryngopharynx
hyoid bone
esophagus
thyroid cartilage (Adam's apple)
vocal fold
cricoid cartilage
thyroid gland
trachea

epiglottis

view of laryngeal
inlet from above

vocal folds

adducted (speaking position)   *Vocal Cords*   abducted (breathing position)

Upper portion of the respiratory system, showing the pharynx and larynx.

reason, if a foreign object such as a peanut escapes the flap of the epiglottis and is inhaled, it usually rolls down the trachea into the right lung. This can cause all or part of the lung to collapse. The object can be removed by a surgical procedure known as bronchoscopy.

The epithelium of the trachea and larger bronchi consists of mucus-producing cells and of cells that contain fine hairs called cilia. When infectious particles or noxious gases such as cigarette smoke elude the first line of defense in the nose, mucus forms in large amounts, trapping many of the particles. Then mucus, foreign particles, and dead epithelial cells combine into sputum, which is caught by the cilia and pushed upward where it can be coughed out of the respiratory tract.

The lungs, a pair of expandable elastic organs, bring oxygen into the body and rid it of carbon dioxide. These vital organs surround the heart, the main artery, the main vein, and the esophagus. The lungs are covered by two layers of tissue called the visceral (inner) and pectoral (outer) pleura.

Each lung contains major subdivisions called lobes, 3 on the right and 2 on the left, and the lobes are divided into bronchopulmonary segments—10 in each lung. These segments are subdivided into increasingly smaller bronchi that eventually taper into the alveoli—grapelike clusters of air sacs where gas exchange (the interchange of oxygen and carbon dioxide) actually occurs.

Two large veins, the superior and inferior vena cavae, drain deoxygenated blood from the body into the right side of the heart, which then pumps the blood into the lungs through the many branches of the pulmonary artery. As the smallest branches of these veins (capillaries) pass by the alveoli, carbon dioxide leaves the blood and oxygen enters it. The newly oxygenated blood then circulates to the left side of the heart by way of the pulmonary vein and is pushed out into the body by the aorta.

The last crucial segment of the respiratory tract is the ear. It is divided into three major parts:

- The external ear, composed of the pinna (the part of the ear sticking out of the side of the head) and the external part of the ear canal, including the tympanic membrane (eardrum).

- The middle ear, the space behind the tympanic membrane that contains the ossicles, three tiny bones that transmit sound waves from the outside world toward the brain.

- The inner ear, which contains the structures used for balance and hearing.

The external ear canal is lined by skin containing special sweat glands that produce wax. Other cells in the external ear canal have hairs. Wax and hair cells work in combination to filter out large particles and push them out of the ear.

The middle ear is full of air. Air pressure is balanced within this chamber via the eustachian tube, a narrow canal connecting the middle ear to the nasopharynx, in the throat. Many nerves course through the entire ear, making it a remarkably delicate and sensitive organ. The ear pain felt during airplane flights is usually caused by an increase in pressure in the middle ear.

(continued from page 54)

Pharyngitis and Tonsillitis

Sore throat (pharyngitis) is usually a viral illness, often accompanied by inflammation and tonsillitis (infection of the tonsils). Throat infections caused by bacteria are most often caused by group A beta-hemolytic *Streptococcus*, the organism that causes strep throat.

Strep throat, a common infection in children over two years of age, is characterized by severe sore throat, fever, malaise, and—sometimes—by abdominal pain. The tonsils usually enlarge and are covered with pus. A culture of the pus will then reveal group A beta-hemolytic strep. Strep throat is easily treated with penicillin or erythromycin.

Routine complications include sinusitis and otitis media. More severe complications include glomerulonephritis (inflammation of the kidneys that usually heals on its own) and rheumatic fever (inflammation and subsequent damage to heart valves). Rheumatic fever is usually prevented by early and complete treatment of strep throat. Glomerulonephritis cannot be prevented.

Croup and Epiglottitis

Croup (angina trachealis) is a viral illness common among young children. It is usually caused by the parainfluenza viruses. Inflammation of the larynx, trachea, and large bronchi cause a narrowing of the air passages, resulting in stridor (noisy inhalation) and general difficulty breathing. The cough accompanying croup is described as "barking" because it sounds like the noise made by a dog or seal.

Croup usually clears up in a few days; the best treatment is cool mist from a vaporizer or cool night air. Children with severe croup may need to be hospitalized so they can immediately be given medication or undergo surgery if the swelling of the airways causes dangerously labored breathing.

Epiglottitis, or inflammation and infection of the epiglottis, is a life-threatening illness almost always caused by *Haemophilus influenzae* type B. This disorder causes the epiglottis to become so swollen that it completely blocks the airway. A doctor must then insert a breathing tube (an endotracheal tube) in the mouth, down the throat, and into the trachea to bypass the obstructing epiglottis. The tube is removed when the swelling is resolved. In addition to opening the airway, treatment may include intravenous antibiotics.

Bronchiolitis

Bronchiolitis, a viral infection of the lower respiratory tract, often strikes infants and young children. It occurs when air is trapped in the alveoli (air sacs) because small branches of the bronchi become inflamed and infected. When the child forceably tries to exhale in order to push this trapped air out of the small airways, he or she ends up wheezing. The most common infectious agent in bronchiolitis is respiratory syncytial virus (RSV), which merely causes a cold in older children and adults.

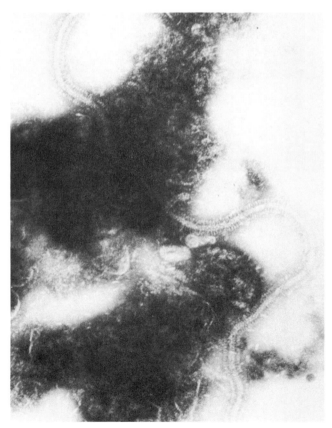

Microscopic view of a respiratory syncytial virus (RSV), which is usually to blame for infections of the lower respiratory tract, including bronchiolitis and some forms of the common cold.

Most young children tolerate bronchiolitis well, and the disease clears up in a few days. Infants with heart and lung abnormalities and those born prematurely, however, can become dangerously ill when infected with RSV.

Bronchitis

Bronchitis is another disease of the lower respiratory tract, often complicating a URI. It strikes when the large and small branches of the bronchial tree become inflamed and infected. A person with bronchitis produces a lot of sputum and coughs a great deal. Generally, it is a viral illness. Sometimes, however, it means that a bacterial superinfection after a viral URI has occurred. In this case, antibiotic treatment is required.

Pneumonia

Pneumonia is the inflammation and infection of the lung, striking specifically the branches of the bronchial tree and the interstitial tissues of the lung. It is a fairly common infection in children, somewhat less common in young adults, and very common in the elderly. Unlike bronchiolitis and bronchitis, pneumonia has many causes, including viruses, bacteria, fungi, or an organism called *Mycoplasma pneumoniae*, a cross between a virus and a bacterium. Bacterial pneumonia may be associated with bacteremia (the presence of bacteria in the blood).

Signs and symptoms of pneumonia vary with both the type of microorganism involved and the age of the infected person. Infants often suffer from tachypnea (rapid breathing), whereas older children and adults are more likely to experience cough and chest pain.

Viral pneumonia is most commonly caused by parainfluenza virus, influenza virus, adenovirus, or RSV, though it can also occur as a complication of other viral illnesses such as chicken pox or measles. Its victims are usually infants and young children. The inflammation of the lung tissue occurs in patches throughout the lungs. A chest X ray routinely shows many white patches (normal lung tissue appears black on an X ray), which represent diffuse inflammation.

Bacterial pneumonia, on the other hand, can either be a diffuse process or involve one or more whole lobes, a condition called lobar pneumonia. It may be preceded by a viral URI. In children, *Streptococcus pneumoniae* and *Haemophilus influenzae* type B are the bacterial organisms that most commonly cause pneumonia. *Staphylococcus aureus* can produce a severe form of pneumonia that may actually destroy lung tissue. Antibiotic therapy is necessary to treat bacterial pneumonia. In lobar pneumonia, the X ray shows one or more solid-white lobes.

Mycoplasma generally causes a diffuse pneumonia. It is most common in teenagers and young adults, though it also infects young children. Signs and symptoms vary from cough and low-grade fever (sometimes referred to as "walking pneumonia") to the whole group of symptoms seen in flulike illnesses. Even if the patient receives antibiotics, the symptoms may last for weeks.

Alexander Fleming, early 1930s. The British physician discovered penicillin, the antibiotic that has proved miraculously effective against bacteria that cause flu, pneumonia, and other illnesses.

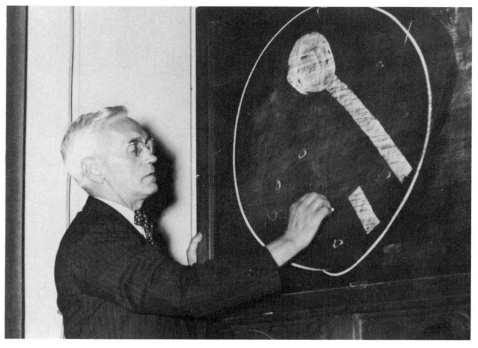

A rather unusual way to contract pneumonia is to aspirate (inhale) one's stomach contents or a foreign body, such as a toy or peanut. This usually happens when someone vomits while lying on his or her back and gravity pulls the fluid into the upper lobes of the lung. Aspirating stomach contents and saliva causes a mixed bacterial infection that usually involves the upper lobes. Pneumonia from aspiration of a foreign body, on the other hand, most likely involves the middle or lower lobe of the right lung. The foreign body becomes stuck in a relatively large branch of the bronchial tree, and fluid collects behind it, making the area susceptible to infection. All aspiration pneumonias require antibiotic therapy. Foreign bodies in the lung must be surgically removed.

•   •   •   •

CHAPTER 5

THE GASTROINTESTINAL TRACT

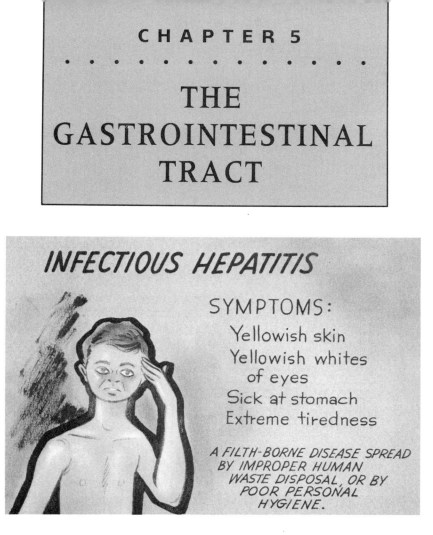

Sometimes, in the middle of the night, one's stomach becomes so cramped that a sound sleep ends dramatically. For the next 12 to 24 hours, or longer, one suffers an agonizing cycle of diarrhea, vomiting, pain, chills, fever, and headache. This is a classic case of gastroenteritis, or stomach flu.

The term *gastroenteritis* refers to a wide variety of viral, bacterial, or parasitic infections. Such an infection can end in a day or linger until it becomes life threatening. In fact, dehydration from gastrointestinal infections is still among the leading killers of children in developing countries.

INFECTIONS OF THE GASTROINTESTINAL TRACT

Except for infections of the respiratory tract, those of the gastrointestinal (GI) tract are probably the most common ailments among children and adults. They are generally caused by virus, but sometimes gastroenteritis is a bacterial or even a parasitic disease. Microorganisms that cause gastroenteritis are often passed from person to person by the fecal-oral route; the feces of an infected person or animal contaminates the food or hands of another person, transmitting the disease. This usually happens when people with diarrhea shed these microorganisms, which then stay alive on their skin or clothing and are passed to another person. Gastroenteritis is characterized by diarrhea and sometimes by vomiting and fever.

Diarrhea is the result of rapid transit of chyme through the intestinal tract. (Chyme, a semiliquid, acid mass, is the form in which food passes from the stomach to the small intestine.) The chyme goes through so quickly that the body does not have enough time to reabsorb water and electrolytes. The result is abnormally high water content in the stools and, potentially, an imbalance of electrolytes in the body.

Vomiting occurs when peristalsis, the normal waves of muscular contraction throughout the gut, is inhibited by paralysis or reverse peristalsis. The stomach then becomes distended with partially digested food and with the ever-present gastric juices; when the stomach cannot empty because of the lack of normal peristalsis, it empties in reverse via the esophagus, pharynx, and mouth.

Viral Gastroenteritis

By far the most common cause of viral gastroenteritis is the rotavirus. If it invades someone's small intestine, he or she suffers watery diarrhea for about a week, often accompanied by vomiting, abdominal cramping, and fever. Rotavirus chiefly attacks small children.

Another common GI virus is called Norwalk, named after Norwalk, Ohio, where the first identifiable outbreak occurred. This virus may cause more vomiting than diarrhea, as well as fever, cramps, and malaise.

When a virus invades the small intestine, one result is large quantities of electrolytes and water in the stool, which have failed to be reabsorbed along the way. This can result in dehydration, a decrease in the total amount of water in the body. Many of the enzymes used in the metabolism of proteins and sugars are also temporarily destroyed. Dehydration can often be prevented if the patient is fed special, balanced electrolyte solutions that contain appropriate amounts of sodium, potassium, chloride, bicarbonate, glucose, and water. If vomiting prevents oral rehydration, or if the disease has lasted so long that oral rehydration will be inadequate, fluids and electrolytes can be replaced intravenously.

Bacterial Gastroenteritis

Bacterial agents that commonly cause GI illnesses include *Salmonella*, *Shigella*, *Staphylococcus*, *Campylobacter*, *Yersinia*, and certain strains of *Escherichia coli*. Crowded living situations, poor sanitary conditions (particularly a lack of clean water), and malnutrition often contribute to the spread of these bacteria, and as a result, the incidence of bacterial gastroenteritis is high in developing nations.

Salmonella *Salmonella* bacteria can appear in even the cleanest places if scrupulous hygienic precautions are not taken. Sometimes, without knowing it, one may swallow contaminated food or drink. Sometimes one eats poultry, eggs, and meat that have not been fully washed and cooked, and these can be the most common sources of bacteria. Someone who carries the virus may contaminate the food they prepare and so pass it to others. Many children have been exposed to *Salmonella* by playing with infected pet turtles, then putting their hands in their mouths without first washing them.

In very young children and in the elderly, *Salmonella* may invade the bloodstream and the GI tract, but most others are stricken when *Salmonella* invades the small and sometimes the large intestine, where it produces a toxin that induces diarrhea, usually preceded by fever, nausea, vomiting, and abdominal cramps. In rare cases, *Salmonella* has caused pneumonia, meningitis, or septic arthritis. Someone who develops any of these complications must take antibiotics, although a mild case is generally treated only with oral or intravenous rehydration.

(continued on page 68)

The Gastrointestinal Tract

The gastrointestinal (GI) tract breaks down and absorbs food and eliminates solid waste. It also protects the body from some poisons and helps defend it against certain infections by forming immunoglobulins.

Food enters the GI tract at the lips and is broken down by being chewed and then mixing with saliva. Saliva, produced by the salivary glands in the mouth, contains the enzymes (proteins that break down various substances) that aid in the early stages of digestion.

Taste buds in the tongue alert the body if food is spoiled or tastes bad, so it can be spit out before digestion proceeds. Once food passes the taste stage, muscles in the tongue and pharynx contract and cause it to be swallowed and pushed down through the oropharynx toward the esophagus. This is a tube 23 to 25 centimeters long that joins the head and neck to the abdomen. Rhythmic contractions of the muscles in the esophagus, known as peristaltic waves, push the mushy chunks of chewed food mixed with saliva down the esophagus and into the stomach.

The stomach digests and stores food. An expandable bag, it can hold as much as two to three quarts of partially digested food and fluid. Its mucosal lining contains a variety of specialized cells that produce the various elements of gastric juice, the fluid that breaks down food products into smaller components.

Peristaltic waves in the stomach push the watery concoction of nearly digested food and gastric juice, called chyme (pronounced *kime*), toward the duodenum, the first part of the small intestine. Here it is broken down and absorbed still further.

The stomach produces its own enzymes and other small molecules used for the middle stage of digestion, but the small intestine depends on the liver, gallbladder, and pancreas to help it in the final stage of the digestive process.

The pancreas lies below the stomach, amid the curves of the small intestine. It actually has two separate functions. It makes digestive enzymes that are secreted into the duodenum by the main pancreatic duct and it makes hormones that control the metabolism of carbohydrates secreted directly into the blood.

Pancreatic enzymes figure in the late stages of digestion of proteins, fats, and starches. Once these enzymes and others from the small intestine have acted on

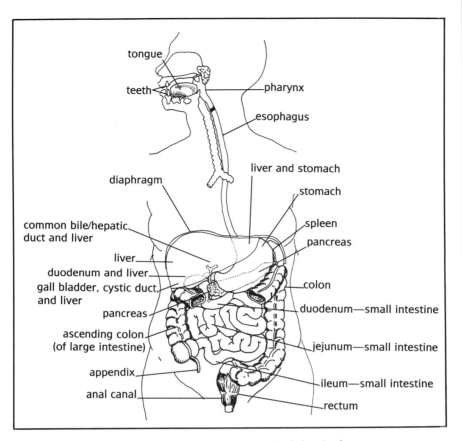

Diagram of the digestive system. Diarrhea and abdominal cramps are common symptoms of microbial infection.

the chyme from the stomach, food is broken down into components small enough to be absorbed by the cells lining the small intestine.

The liver, in the right upper abdomen, is another multipurpose organ. First, it produces bile, a liquid stored in the gallbladder and released into the duodenum via the common bile duct. Bile is crucial for the digestion and absorption of fats. Second, the liver stores many of the broken down products of the digestive process for later use by the body. Third, it forms and stores vitamins and blood-clotting factors. Fourth, it performs the detoxification and excretion of substances such as alcohol and the toxic by-products of normal metabolism such as ammonia.

(continued from page 65)

Shigella   The invasive bacterium *Shigella* causes a severe form of diarrhea called dysentery, characterized by frequent stools full of blood and mucus. The disease is usually passed directly from one person to another, but it can be caused by contaminated food or water. The bacterium produces a toxin that may not be an essential component of the GI part of the disease. Once *Shigella* invades the mucosa, or mucous membrane, of the colon, huge numbers of white blood cells enter the victim's stools.

Shigella dysentery is almost always accompanied by high fever and severe abdominal cramps. Complications include dehydration and seizures. Although the infection will eventually clear up on its own, antibiotics can speed the patient's recovery.

Staphylococcus Aureus   Food poisoning by *Staphylococcus aureus* causes a short-lived but violent bacterial gastroenteritis. The foods usually responsible are dairy products—milk, cream, eggs, and such—that have not been properly refrigerated. This type of food poisoning is well known for attacking picnickers who leave their potato salad in an uncooled basket for four or more hours. Staphylococcal food poisoning may be to blame if a person vomits profusely and is plagued with diarrhea one to eight hours after eating. The victim rarely is dehydrated and usually recovers without medication in a day or two.

Campylobacter Jejuni   The bacterium *Campylobacter jejuni* causes fever, abdominal cramps, and bloody diarrhea. The organism, which is passed on by a person, cat, dog, or by contaminated food or water, usually attacks the small intestine and the colon. White blood cells are commonly found in the stools. *Campylobacter* gastroenteritis clears up on its own in about a week but is usually treated with antibiotics.

Yersinia Enterocolitica   The bacterium *Yersinia enterocolitica* causes diarrhea and sometimes abdominal pain so severe it is easily mistaken for acute appendicitis. The stools contain mucus but rarely blood. The disease may last two to three weeks; antibiotics are generally not required.

Escherichia Coli   Certain strains of the normal gut flora *Escherichia coli* (commonly written *E. coli*) have been shown to

The Small Intestine

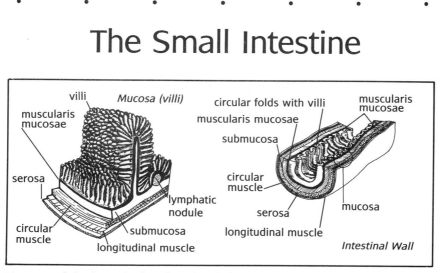

villi   *Mucosa (villi)*   circular folds with villi   muscularis mucosae

muscularis mucosae   muscularis mucosae

submucosa

serosa   circular muscle

lymphatic nodule

circular muscle   submucosa   serosa   mucosa

longitudinal muscle   longitudinal muscle

Intestinal Wall

Diagram of the intestinal wall and a close-up of the mucosa. By absorbing and secreting water and other fluids, the mucosa help to block the passage of some disease-causing microorganisms.

The small intestine completes the body's digestion and absorption of nutrients. Though tightly coiled, it is about 13 feet long and is divided into three sections: the duodenum, the jejunum, and the ileum.

The mucosal lining of the small intestine consists of thousands of folds, called villi. During normal function of the small intestine, electrolytes (sodium, potassium, chloride, and bicarbonate) and water are absorbed and secreted by the cells on the surface of the villi. The absorption of amino acids (the components of protein), fatty acids and glycerol (the substances that result from the digestion of fats), and glucose from the small intestine is facilitated by water and electrolyte transport.

The small and large intestines intersect near the appendix. For centuries, anatomists thought the appendix served no purpose. Now many researchers believe the appendix plays a role—as yet unknown—in the immune system.

The colon, part of the large intestine, receives what remains of the chyme that has not been absorbed in the small intestine. Some remaining nutrients can be absorbed by the colonic mucosa, but the primary purpose of the colon is to reabsorb as much water and as many electrolytes as possible. It leaves behind only the solid waste products, called feces. Peristalsis propels the feces, which are lubricated by mucus from the colon's lining, into the rectum (the last part of the large intestine) and out of the body via the anus.

cause gastroenteritis. Some strains produce bloody diarrhea. Others, which produce toxins, are now believed to be the bacteria that most commonly causes "traveler's diarrhea." This type of gastroenteritis is characterized by profuse watery diarrhea, nausea, and cramping, and, in many instances, fever. Antibiotics help clear up the symptoms.

PARASITIC GASTROENTERITIS

One of the most common intestinal parasites is *Giardia lamblia*. It can be swallowed in contaminated drinking water or passed from person to person. The organism lands in the small intestine. It can cause diarrhea that lasts for many weeks, and during this time the victim may have great difficulty absorbing sugars and fats. *Giardia* responds very well to drug therapy.

HEPATITIS

Hepatitis, the inflammation and infection of the liver, is caused by a wide variety of viral agents. It may be a complication of a systemic viral illness such as cytomegalovirus, herpes, various enterovirus infections, and Epstein-Barr virus. More commonly, however, the viruses responsible for hepatitis are those designated hepatitis A, hepatitis B, or non-A, non-B hepatitis.

Hepatitis A (HA) is generally transmitted from person to person. Epidemics are often traced to contaminated water or shellfish, and they are also common in day-care centers. Signs and symptoms of HA include fever, malaise, nausea, vomiting, diarrhea, and loss of appetite. Another symptom, liver inflammation, obstructs the flow of bile from that organ to the gallbladder, causing the fluid to be absorbed into the bloodstream and deposited in the urine and in the skin. This development, called jaundice, gives the skin a yellow tint. Hepatitis A tends to be a mild disease. It usually lasts about two weeks and clears up without complications.

Hepatitis B (HB) is generally transmitted by contact with blood. Infection can occur when the blood, saliva, semen, or vaginal secretions of an infected person come into contact with breaks in the skin or mucous membranes. Before adequate testing was available, people often caught HB during blood trans-

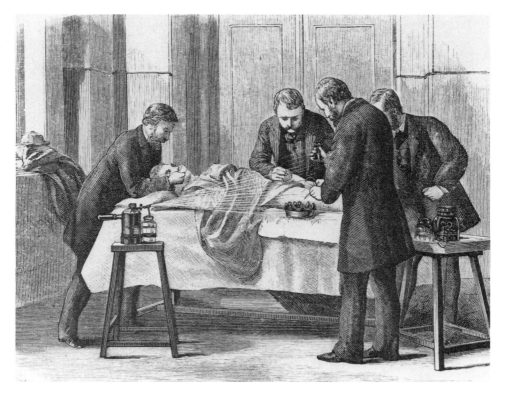

An 1882 engraving shows Joseph Lister's early procedure for antisepsis, the creation of a germ-free environment: spraying carbolic acid. Improper protection, even during surgery, can allow hepatitis and other diseases to spread.

fusions. Now it is passed on during sexual intercourse; by intravenous drug users who share needles; by contaminated needles with which health-care workers accidentally stick themselves; and from mother to child during the third trimester of pregnancy.

As with HA, HB tends to be a milder disease in younger people than in adults. Symptoms are similar to those that appear in HA, but the disease usually lasts a month or more. Possible complications include irreversible liver damage, which can lead to death, or to a chronic case of hepatitis in which the disease never completely disappears. Children who have had HB run the risk of eventually developing hepatocellular carcinoma, a liver cancer, or other liver diseases. People at risk for HB because of known exposure to the disease or frequent exposure to blood (doctors, nurses, dentists, lab workers, and others) can obtain vaccinations.

Another form of hepatitis, known as non-A, non-B, is responsible for the majority of cases that result from blood transfusion. People who are infected with non-A, non-B hepatitis have a high risk of developing chronic hepatitis and irreversible liver damage. Because the virus responsible for this strain has not yet been identified, no specific treatment is available.

•　　　•　　　•　　　•

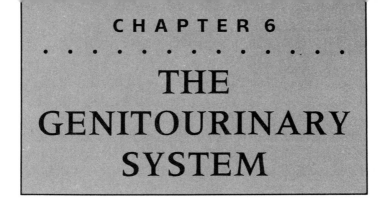

CHAPTER 6

· · · · · · · · · · · · · ·

THE GENITOURINARY SYSTEM

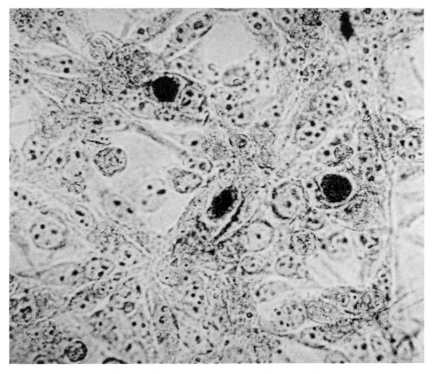

Tissue culture of Chlamydia trachomatis *(dark spots) in urinary tract.*

The genitourinary system consists of the urinary tract and the reproductive tract. Infections of the reproductive organs, caused by many bacteria, viruses, fungi, and parasites, are generally passed by sexual contact. In women, complications of these sexually transmitted diseases (STDs) can impair the ability to bear children.

INFECTIONS OF THE URINARY TRACT

Bladder infections are technically called cystitis but more often referred to as urinary tract infections (UTIs). They occur fairly often in young children, adolescent or young-adult females, and in elderly or disabled people. During the newborn period, males and females are equally susceptible to UTIs, but thereafter, females are 10 times more likely to develop a UTI, probably because the female's urethra, which is shorter than the male's, provides an easier pathway for bacteria to travel as they ascend toward the bladder.

The bacteria responsible for UTIs are found naturally in the colon. *Escherichia coli* accounts for up to 90% of UTIs; other common organisms include those from the genera *Pseudomonas*, *Klebsiella*, *Proteus*, and streptococcus D from the enterococci group.

Symptoms of UTIs vary with the age of the infected person. Newborn babies show generalized signs of illness—fever, lethargy, irritability, poor feeding, and vomiting. Their infections usually occur first in the blood and then in the urinary tract. Older infants may suffer fever, abdominal pain, vomiting, and diarrhea, and may dribble foul-smelling urine rather than produce a normal urinary stream. After infancy, UTIs are charac-

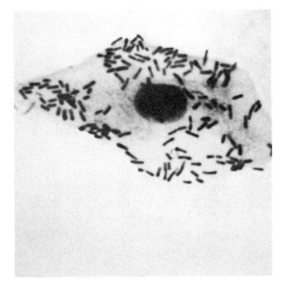

This microscopic view of an infected epithelial cell in the urinary tract shows dozens of Escherichia coli *bacteria adhering near the cell wall. The mass at center is the cell nucleus.*

The Urinary Tract

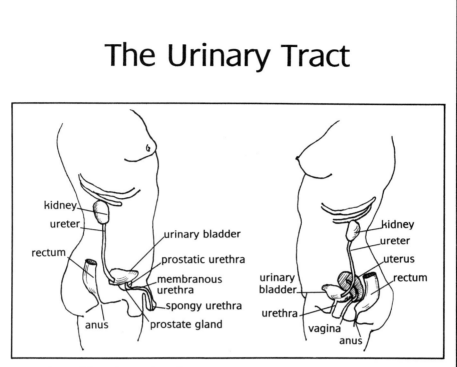

The male and female genitourinary tracts.

From the kidneys to the bladder, the urinary tract is essentially the same in males and females. However, the urethra, the tube that drains urine from the bladder out of the body, is set up differently in each sex. The kidneys filter all the blood in the body, regulating the amount of water and electrolytes in the blood and removing toxic by-products. The end product is urine.

Filtration of the blood begins in the glomeruli, thousands of clusters of capillaries located in the kidneys. Each glomerulus is attached to a long twisted structure called a tubule, where electrolytes and water are exchanged. The tubules meet at the kidney area called the renal pelvis, where urine is collected for excretion.

Each kidney is connected to the bladder by its ureter, a long, narrow, muscular tube. Peristaltic waves help the flow of urine toward the bladder, an expandable muscular bag that stores urine and then excretes it through the urethra.

The male urethra is 15 to 20 centimeters long, extending from the bladder through the penis. The female urethra is only two to six centimeters long, from the bladder almost to the vagina.

One of the first electron microscopes, early 1950s. These machines have proved indispensable to researchers who investigate the microbial world, including the nature of sexually transmitted diseases.

terized by a burning sensation during urination, by frequent urination, and by an inability to hold urine in the bladder. The urine may also be foul smelling.

Examination of the urine will reveal bacteria, white blood cells, and sometimes red blood cells. A culture of the urine will grow large numbers of the bacteria responsible for the disease. Uncomplicated UTIs are easily treated with oral antibiotics.

The presence of UTIs in young children may signal a problem in their urinary tract. One example may be the occurrence of tiny holes joining the bladder and the colon. Another may be abnormalities in the structure and function of the ureters (tubes that carry urine from kidneys to the urethra) or of the urethra itself. X-ray studies are very useful in defining structural abnormalities. Proper treatment at an early age helps reduce the chance of severe kidney problems later in life.

Pyelonephritis

If the bacteria in the bladder ascend the ureters and infect the kidneys, the result is pyelonephritis. Its signs and symptoms include fever, pain in the sides of the abdomen, and vomiting. Bacteria and white blood cells become present in the urine, and a culture will grow the same bacteria that cause simple UTIs.

Recurrent pyelonephritis can cause scarring of the kidneys and lead over time to irreversible kidney damage. Oral antibiotics are not an effective treatment for pyelonephritis. It is best treated intravenously.

SEXUALLY TRANSMITTED DISEASES

Most diseases of the male and female genital tracts are transmitted by sexual contact. Infection during pregnancy can be dangerous for the developing fetus; repeated infections can impair the ability to bear children. The best way to prevent these infections is to use condoms.

Herpesvirus Hominis (HVH) Herpesvirus hominis is responsible for genital herpes. Like its relative, the varicella virus, HVH can exist in a dormant state after the initial infection and reappear over and over again. During the active phase of infection, the virus can be passed to sexual partners and, in childbirth, to newborn babies. In women, lesions generally appear on the cervix, vagina, and vulva; in men, on the penis. In some cases, the antiviral agent acyclovir will shorten the period of viral shedding, but it does not eradicate the infection.

Gonorrhea Gonorrhea is caused by the bacterium *Neisseria gonorrhoeae* and is currently the second most common sexually transmitted disease in the world. The infection can be introduced into the cervix, urethra, anus, throat, or eyes and can spread to all of the male and female reproductive organs, the skin, joints, brain, spinal cord, and heart.

Gonorrhea was reliably treated with penicillin until recently, when resistant strains of the bacteria developed. New drugs such as ceftriaxone have emerged to treat these strains.

The Female Reproductive Tract

The female reproductive tract is a system of organs responsible for the maturation of ova (eggs), the growth and development of the fetus, and the production of some of the female hormones.

A woman has two ovaries. At birth, each ovary contains about 200,000 follicles, each of which is an ovum (a single, at this point, immature egg) surrounded by a layer of epithelial tissue. Unlike the male testes, which constantly produce sperm, all of the eggs available for use are present at the time a female baby is born.

The ovaries are loosely attached to the uterus by the broad ligaments and the ovarian ligaments. Each ovary is filled with ova in various stages of development. Approximately every 28 days one ovum from one ovary passes through all of its phases of development and leaves the ovary to begin the journey to the uterus. A few others begin the maturation process every month, but those that do not complete the process will degenerate.

Ovulation, the rupturing of a follicle with release of its ovum, occurs in the middle of the approximately 28-day menstrual cycle. For approximately the next 24 hours the ovum is available for fertilization (combination with a sperm). The remainder of the follicle forms the corpus luteum, which makes the female hormone progesterone.

Once it is released from an ovary, the ovum is picked up by a fallopian tube (also known as an oviduct or a uterine tube), a hollow structure emptying into the uterus. The ovarian end of the fallopian tube is attached to the ovary by fingerlike folds of its mucosa, called fimbriae. If fertilization occurs, it happens in the fallopian tube; to reach the ovum, sperm must travel through the vagina, the cervix, the uterus, and up into the fallopian tube.

The uterus has two major parts: the body, where the fallopian tubes are attached, and the cervix, located within the vagina. The uterus is a muscular organ, full of blood vessels. During the menstrual cycle the lining of the uterus (the endometrium) becomes thickened and the blood vessels grow new branches to supply the developing endometrium.

If pregnancy does not occur, the endometrium sheds during menstruation, exiting the body via the cervix and vagina. If pregnancy does occur, the endometrium helps to nourish the embryo during its earliest stages.

The vagina is a hollow, expandable space with a muscular component in its walls and an epithelial lining that is very much like skin. During sexual intercourse the vagina is lubricated by glands that line its opening; during the birth process the cervix and the vagina stretch, allowing the baby to leave the uterus.

Three elements of the female reproductive system.

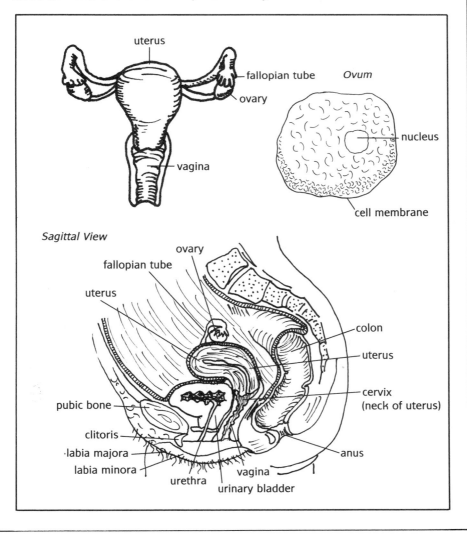

uterus
fallopian tube
ovary
vagina

Ovum
nucleus
cell membrane

Sagittal View
ovary
fallopian tube
uterus
pubic bone
clitoris
labia majora
labia minora
urethra
urinary bladder
vagina
colon
uterus
cervix
(neck of uterus)
anus

The Male Reproductive Tract

The male reproductive tract is composed of the testes, the penis, and a series of ducts and glands. The testes are located outside the body in a sac of skin called the scrotum. Their exterior location is significant because sperm, in order to mature, need a cooler temperature than the body normally maintains. The testes have a variety of functions, including production of sperm and the male hormones responsible for the development of male characteristics.

Sperm are formed in an area of the testes called the seminiferous tubules. The tubules are made up of specialized cells that protect and nourish the maturing sperm. Other cells in the surrounding interstitial tissue are responsible for making male hormones. Sperm make their way to the outside world through a series of ducts: the tubuli recti, the rete testes, and the ductuli efferentes. These last empty into the epididymis, a structure that lies on top of each testicle. Sperm are stored in the epididymis, allowed to mature, and propelled out by ejaculation.

The ductus deferens is the next part of the path from the testes to the penis. It passes up from the epididymis and into the abdomen as part of the spermatic cord, a collection of blood vessels, nerves, muscle fibers, and the ductus deferens. Contractions of the muscle fibers help push sperm toward the penis. As the ductus deferens passes by the bladder, it widens and also receives fluid formed in the seminal vesicle, an outpouching of the ductus deferens responsible for much of the fluid part of semen.

As the ductus deferens passes through the prostate it opens into the urethra via the ejaculatory duct. The prostate contains glands that contribute fluid to the semen. From this point on, semen takes the same path as urine, exiting the body via the urethra.

The penis is made up of three masses of spongy tissue, a pair of corpora cavernosa, and the single corpus spongiosum, through which the urethra passes. During erection this spongy tissue fills with blood and becomes stiff; after ejaculation the blood drains back into the venous system and the penis becomes flaccid.

Three elements of the male reproductive system.

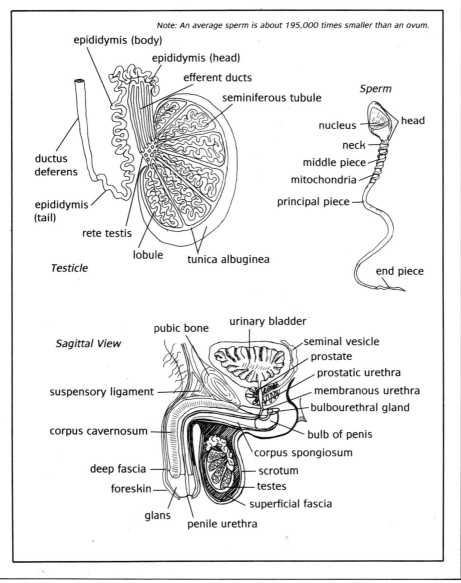

Note: An average sperm is about 195,000 times smaller than an ovum.

epididymis (body)
epididymis (head)
efferent ducts
seminiferous tubule

ductus deferens

epididymis (tail)

rete testis

lobule
tunica albuginea

Testicle

Sperm

nucleus — head
neck
middle piece
mitochondria
principal piece

end piece

Sagittal View

pubic bone
urinary bladder
seminal vesicle
prostate
prostatic urethra

suspensory ligament
membranous urethra
bulbourethral gland

corpus cavernosum
bulb of penis
corpus spongiosum

deep fascia
scrotum

foreskin
testes

glans
superficial fascia

penile urethra

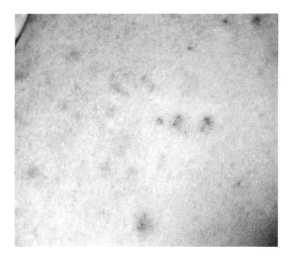

Skin of a person with secondary syphilis. The bacterial infection, usually acquired through sexual intercourse, begins with a sore in the genital area, then spreads as a rash.

(continued from page 77)

Chlamydia The only sexually transmitted disease more common than gonorrhea is chlamydia. It is frequently passed from infected mothers to their newborn children, causing pneumonia and conjunctivitis (eye infections). Chlamydia, an inflammation caused by infection, affects all the organs in the male and female genital tracts and often strikes at the same time as gonorrhea. Some antibiotics can lessen its symptons.

Syphilis The bacterium responsible for syphilis, another STD, is *Treponema pallidum*. Syphilis is acquired through sexual contact, contaminated blood or needles, and by passage from pregnant women to their unborn children. It had ceased to be a common ailment in the middle of this century but then resurfaced in the mid-1980s, when a huge number of cases were reported. Its spread may be related to the spread of AIDS, which is passed from person to person by similar routes.

Infants born with syphilis—a condition known as congenital syphilis—suffer a variety of skin lesions. In addition, the mucous membranes of the nose, mouth, and genitalia are affected. The disease also attacks the liver, spleen, bones, and bone marrow. Deformities known as saddle nose, Hutchinson's teeth (narrowed and notched permanent incisions), and mulberry molars commonly occur. In fact, congenital syphilis can infect any organ.

The form of syphilis seen in adolescents and adults begins with a single painful sore in the genital area, which eventually turns into a small ulcer known as a chancre. Without treatment, the disease progresses to a systemic illness that resembles influenza.

During this stage, a rash develops that may cover the entire body and involve the mucous membranes. The disease may enter a latent (inactive) phase and then reappear after a number of years in any organ system, particularly in the central nervous system. If diagnosed properly, syphilis is easily treated with penicillin.

AIDS Acquired immune deficiency syndrome is a viral illness transmitted by sexual contact, by infected pregnant women to their unborn children, or by contact with contaminated blood products. This last means of exposure can occur accidentally, such as when health-care workers stick themselves with contaminated needles, or by transfusions of contaminated blood products. By 1988, the majority of Americans newly afflicted with the disease were intravenous drug users who acquired the infection by sharing needles. Elsewhere in the world, however, sexual intercourse is the main avenue of infection.

AIDS is caused by the human immunodeficiency virus (HIV). The illness that follows is indistinguishable from many other common viral illnesses. During a period that may last only a few

Diagram of HIV (human immunodeficiency virus), which causes AIDS. Because it is a retrovirus that can lie dormant for years, finding a vaccine for it is proving difficult.

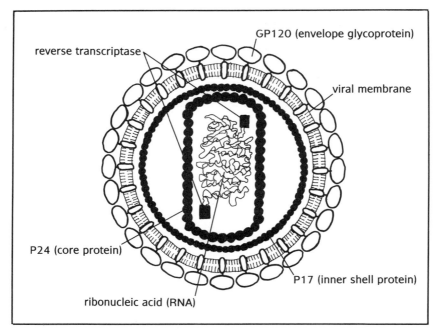

months or as long as three to five years, the virus gradually destroys the immune system, leaving the infected person vulnerable to many bacterial, viral, fungal, and parasitic infections, as well as to certain unusual forms of cancer, such as Kaposi's sarcoma, which covers the victim's skin with red or violet blotches. This battery of diseases ultimately proves deadly.

Many drug treatments are currently being investigated, but no cure for AIDS had been developed as of early 1989. It is not yet known whether every individual who carries the virus will eventually succumb to the disease.

Trichomonas Trichomonas is usually transmitted sexually, although cases have been reported in people who are not sexually active. Males infected with trichomonas have no symptoms; females have a vaginal discharge. The parasitic organisms causing the disease can be seen with a microscope in samples of the discharge. Treatment consists of a single dose of metronidazole.

Condyloma Acuminatum Condyloma acuminatum, or venereal warts, is a viral infection causing wartlike lesions around either the external genitalia, the anus, or both. It is treated topically with podophyllin.

•   •   •   •

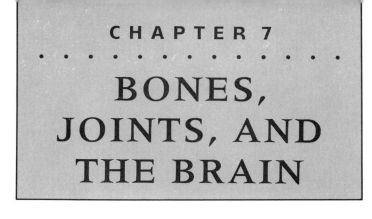

CHAPTER 7

· · · · · · · · · · · ·

BONES, JOINTS, AND THE BRAIN

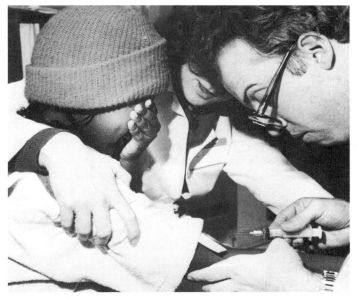

Taking a blood sample during a meningitis outbreak.

Many people think of the skeleton—bones and joints—as simply the frame on which their skin is draped. In fact, the skeleton is an organ system, made up, like any other, of various types of cells, each with a specific function. The skeleton protects the internal organs from injury and gives the human body its form. Certain parts of the skeleton contain the bone marrow where blood cells are formed. Like other organs, the skeleton is susceptible to infection that can alter this normal growth and development. The brain and spinal cord, essential to every motion the body makes, are susceptible to meningitis, a painful and sometimes fatal inflammation.

BONE INFECTIONS

The most common bone infection, osteomyelitis, is usually a childhood disease that can strike nearly any bone in the body. Primarily, though, it is a disease that strikes long bones, such as the femur, tibia, humerus, and radius, as they grow. The infection usually reaches the bone by way of the bloodstream, a process known as hematogenous infection. In most cases, an upper respiratory infection or a bacterial infection from the skin—an infected scratch or pimple—spreads to the bloodstream and is deposited in the metaphysis (the growing portion) of a long bone, setting up a localized infection.

Early signs and symptoms of osteomyelitis include pain and tenderness at the site of the infection, as well as fever and malaise. Later there may be swelling and redness, and pus will form in the infected bone. If the infection is in the leg, the child will limp or be unable to walk at all; if the infection is in the arm, the child

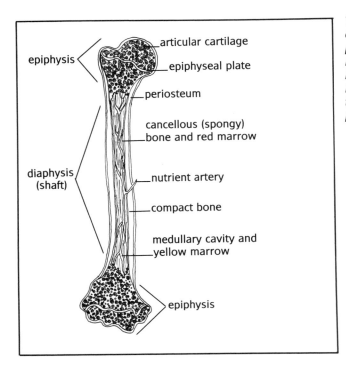

The femur. This and the other long bones are the primary sites for osteomyelitis, usually a childhood disease that can begin with a scratch and then infect the blood and pass to the bones.

may be unwilling to move the arm. Any infection, if left untreated, can spread into the medullary cavity or out through the periosteum and the skin. Sometimes the infection spreads into neighboring joints.

By far the most common organism that produces osteomyelitis is *Staphylococcus aureus*, a type of staph that often lives on the skin and in the respiratory tract. Other causative organisms include *Haemophilus influenzae* type B, pneumococcus, *Salmonella*, and tuberculosis.

When the infection is introduced by a sharp object puncturing the foot, the most common organism is *Pseudomonas aeruginosa*, a bacterium that lives in many damp, dirty places. The infection that may develop after a dog or cat bite is most commonly caused by *Pasteurella multocida*, a bacterium commonly found in cat and dog saliva. Osteomyelitis can also develop after a compound, or open, fracture, in which the ends of a broken bone stick through the skin.

The organism causing a given case of osteomyelitis can usually be identified in a blood culture. Another useful test is a biopsy of the affected bone. A biopsy is a surgical procedure in which a small piece of bone—or any other tissue—is cut out and examined under the microscope and by cultures.

Treatment of osteomyelitis involves a four-to-six-week course of antibiotics given intravenously; sometimes the antibiotics are give intravenously for three to four weeks and thereafter by mouth. In most cases, the infection heals, and new bone grows in to fill the infected area. Occasionally, the area destroyed by the infection is so large that the bone becomes deformed, leaving the limb short.

JOINT INFECTIONS

Like osteomyelitis, septic arthritis, which is a bacterial infection within the joint capsule, most commonly strikes children. As in the case of osteomyelitis, a child with septic arthritis will usually have a fever and resist using the affected limb. When the fluid within the joint becomes infected, pain rapidly ensues, along with tenderness, swelling, and redness. The joint stiffens and becomes warm to the touch.

The organisms most commonly involved in septic arthritis are those that cause osteomyelitis. They can be cultured from the blood or from a sample of the infected joint fluid, which the

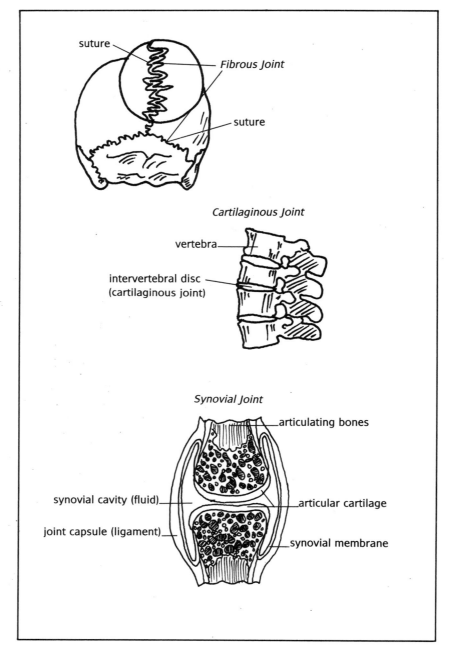

Diagrams of three types of joints. Fluid in the joint capsule is the most likely place for infection to start. Septic arthritis, which mainly strikes children, is one example of a joint infection.

physician collects by sticking a needle in the joint capsule. Treatment of septic arthritis includes intravenous antibiotics and draining of the infected joint fluid by a needle or by surgical incision into the joint space.

Complications can destroy the smooth cartilage that lines the joint. This, in turn, causes permanent deformity and abnormal motion or dislocation of the joint from the pressure of the infected joint fluid. If the dislocation is temporary, it disappears after the infection clears; if it is permanent, it deforms the joint and makes it difficult or impossible for the patient to use the limb. Surgery can help correct this, but the limb will never be the same as before it was infected.

MENINGITIS

Meningitis is an inflammation of the connective tissue membranes that line the skull and vertebral canal and enclose the brain and spinal cord (the meninges). Most commonly, meningitis is bacterial or viral, but it can also be caused by fungal infections, tuberculosis, parasites, and other agents. Noninfectious diseases such as leukemia and brain tumors can also produce meningitis.

Some people—including infants, males, and, possibly, nonwhites—run an especially high risk of contracting the illness. The many varieties of the infection account, in part, for the higher incidence in some groups. Mumps, for instance, which most often affects infants, can be complicated by meningitis. Because the illness usually appears in epidemics, the damage to both the developing child and the population at large is potentially great. Since World War II, however, the rate of fatalities from meningitis in the United States has dropped from about 60% to 5% in cases in which the illness is diagnosed early.

Signs and Symptoms

Signs and symptoms of meningitis, whether caused by a bacterium or a virus, vary according to the age of the victim. Adolescents and adults usually experience a headache, neck pain and stiffness, nausea and vomiting, and photophobia (an abnormal intolerance in which exposure to light produces intense discomfort to the eyes). Infants show subtler signs, such as irritability,

(continued on page 92)

89

Neuroanatomy

The central nervous system consists of the brain and spinal cord. Highly complicated and specialized, the system is responsible for the thoughts, feelings, and actions that differentiate humans from other life forms.

The brain has many subdivisions, each one directing a specific neurologic function or functions. All these areas are interconnected, allowing for smooth integration of normal body functions and behavior. The parts of the brain that control physical activity are connected via the spinal cord to all parts of the body. A different set of connections enables the brain to interpret sensations gathered by the organs of the five senses (touch, taste, smell, sight, and hearing). Other parts of the brain are responsible for speech, judgment, and emotions and tell the body, for example, when to breathe or sleep.

The ventricles are four interconnected spaces within the brain that are filled with cerebrospinal fluid (CSF). A watery material containing a balanced amount of salt, glucose (sugar), and proteins, CSF provides a fluid cushion for the brain. It is constantly being produced by a structure inside the lateral ventricles called the cho-roid plexus. The fluid then circulates through the ventricular system and around the brain and spinal cord, finally being reabsorbed by portions of the meninges.

The meninges are actually three discrete layers of membrane that cover the brain and spinal cord. The outermost meningeal layer, the dura mater, is a thick, fibrous coat for the brain subdivided into two layers. The outer layer attaches to the inner surface of the skull; the inner layer helps divide some of the regions of the brain and contains the large veins that drain blood from the brain.

The middle meningeal layer is called the arachnoid; the innermost layer, which adheres to the brain and spinal cord, is called the pia mater. CSF is present between these two layers, in the subarachnoid space. When the meninges become inflamed and infected—when meningitis occurs—microorganisms, white blood cells (WBCs), and sometimes red blood cells (RBCs) are found in the CSF and pus forms in the subarachnoid space.

Protecting the central nervous system are the skull and the bony part of the spine—the vertebral column, which contains 33 ver-

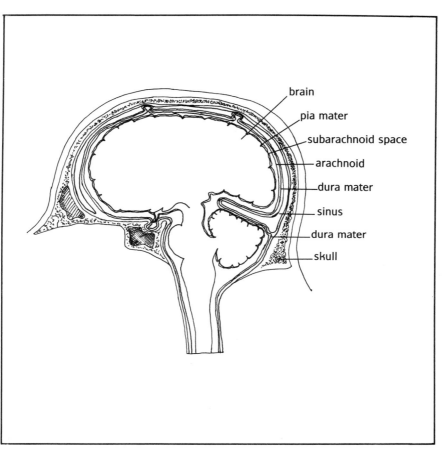

Diagram of the meninges, which include the brain and spinal cord. The bacteria responsible for meningitis, Neisseria meningitidis, will be present in the blood of an infected person.

tebrae: 7 cervical vertebrae in the neck, 12 thoracic vertebrae in the area between the shoulders and the waist (the upper back), and 5 lumbar, 5 sacral, and 4 coccygeal vertebrae in the lower back (below the waist). The sacral and coccygeal vertebrae are usually fused together, forming the coccyx (tailbone).

Fibrous bands called ligaments connect each vertebra to its neighbors above and below. The connections keep all the vertebrae lined up for the twisting and bending the spine must perform.

(continued from page 89)

lethargy, and reduced appetite. Fever, though common, does not occur in every case.

To diagnose meningitis, the physician takes a sample of cerebrospinal fluid (CSF) by means of a lumbar puncture, sometimes called a spinal tap. The doctor inserts a needle through the skin of the patient's lower back and into the subarachnoid space in the gap between the third and fourth or fourth and fifth lumbar vertebrae. (Because the spinal cord stops above this point, the needle will not pierce the cord itself.) A small amount of CSF drips out through the needle and is collected for testing.

The fluid is then cultured in order to grow and identify the offending bacteria or virus. The amount of sugar and protein in the CSF is measured, and the fluid is examined under the microscope for bacteria (viruses cannot be seen through a microscope) and for red and white blood cells.

It is also important to test the blood in order to measure the number and type of its WBCs. Any infection usually elevates the total WBC count; in a bacterial infection there is a predominance of polymorphonuclear cells; in a viral infection, a predominance of lymphocytes and monocytes. Blood cultures are also crucial— in bacterial meningitis the microorganisms responsible for the infection can often be grown from the blood.

In most instances, the infection causing meningitis begins in the upper respiratory tract, producing symptoms of a cold. The microorganism is then carried by the blood to the meninges. It is not necessary to have cold symptoms before developing meningitis, however, and very few colds are complicated by meningitis.

Other, less common pathways for infection of the meninges include direct contact from infected sinuses; from other areas of the head or neck; or even from the skin that overlays the spine. Severe head injuries involving fractures of the skull can create a pathway from the outside world to the meninges and allow introduction of microorganisms into the CSF.

Viral Meningitis

The vast majority of cases of viral meningitis are caused by members of the enterovirus family, particularly the coxsackie viruses and the echovirus. Viral meningitis usually begins as an upper respiratory tract infection. There may be a rash. Sometimes, however, it develops as a complication of infections caused by measles, mumps, rubella, EBV, influenza, chicken pox, herpes, or another virus.

Viruses are difficult to grow in culture. Thus, indirect evidence of a viral infection is important in the diagnosis of viral meningitis. When the CSF is examined, no microorganisms appear, though WBCs are present, primarily lymphocytes and monocytes. The amount of protein will be normal or slightly elevated, and the amount of glucose will be normal or slightly decreased.

Because no specific chemical treatment exists for viral meningitis, therapy aims at controlling headaches and soothing the discomforts of fever, nausea, and vomiting. Sometimes infants and young children—in whom meningitis can be difficult to diagnose—receive intravenous injections of antibiotics for 48 hours while the CSF cultures grow. If no microorganisms are identified, the physician assumes the infection is viral and halts the antibiotic treatment.

Bacterial Meningitis

Bacterial meningitis, sometimes called epidemic meningitis or spotted fever, is more likely than viral meningitis to be a complicated and life-threatening illness. Many factors determine a person's susceptibility to bacterial meningitis.

Epidemiologic evidence—statistical studies based on large populations that do not point to causes but indicate patterns and trends—suggests that children less than two years old are more likely to be affected than older children or adults; boys are more susceptible than girls; and nonwhite children may be more susceptible to infections with certain bacteria than white children. As is the case with most infectious diseases, people with abnormalities of the immune system are at increased risk.

The organisms responsible for bacterial meningitis vary with the age of the affected person. Bacterial meningitis in newborn babies is usually caused by organisms that live in the mother's birth canal and then are passed to the baby during birth, including group B *Streptococcus*, *Escherichia coli*, and *Listeria monocytogenes*. Older infants, toddlers, and school-age children are more often infected by *Haemophilus influenzae* type B, *Neis-*

seria meningitidis, and *Streptococcus pneumoniae*. These bacteria can also cause illness in newborns.

The signs and symptoms of bacterial meningitis are generally the same as those of its viral counterpart. There may be a few days of fever and respiratory symptoms preceding the onset of meningitis, or the disease may have a rapid and severe onset. Additional signs and symptoms that can occur at the outset include seizures, trouble with sight, paralysis, and coma.

Meningitis caused by *Haemophilus influenzae* type B can be a complication of, or can occur in association with, pneumonia, septic arthritis, or cellulitis (an inflammation of the connective tissue between adjacent tissues and organs).

A rash known as purpura, characterized by red-to-purple patches (petechiae) of many sizes caused by bleeding into the skin, is associated with meningococcemia (*Neisseria meningitidis*) but can also be seen with *Haemophilus influenzae* and *Streptococcus pneumoniae*.

A doctor can diagnose bacterial meningitis by examining the CSF. In general, it will contain many WBCs, primarily polymorphonuclear cells. Bacteria may also be seen when the CSF is viewed under a microscope. The protein will be elevated and the glucose depressed—the elevated protein reflects the presence of bacteria in the CSF, and depressed glucose results because it is the energy source bacteria consume while they grow and multiply.

Examination of the blood will reveal an elevated WBC count, with a predominance of polymorphonuclear cells, which is characteristic of bacterial infections. The same bacteria that grows from the CSF is likely to grow from the blood. The illness is treated with antibiotics administered intravenously for 10 to 14 days.

Most people recover completely from all types of meningitis, but some die, and many other complications can result from damage to the brain caused by both the inflammation and the infection. The most common complications include complete or partial deafness, blindness, seizures, paralysis, mental retardation, and difficulties with learning and speech. If there is obstruction of the normal pathways of CSF drainage, the surgical placement of an artificial drain in the brain is required.

•   •   •   •

CHAPTER 8

· · · · · · · · · · · · ·

TOWARD THE FUTURE

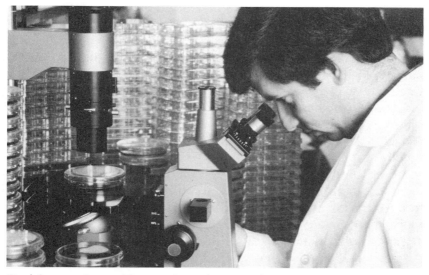

Studying vaccines with a modern electron microscope.

The search to control infectious diseases continues each day, and new breakthroughs occur much more often than in the past. Bacteria and viruses are powerful enemies, however, and it is not likely they will ever be vanquished. Consider the common cold, which not even the most highly advanced technology can defeat. The cold reminds us, no less than do mononucleosis, meningitis, and AIDS, that science cannot instantly crack the shell of every illness, although we sometimes expect it to.

The trouble is it takes a long time not only for researchers to develop cures but also for experiments to verify their effectiveness and safety. A useful example of the pitfalls of research is the case of pertussis, or whooping cough. This ailment, caused by the bacterium *Bordetella pertussis*, causes its victims—most often children—to suffer convulsive bouts of coughing followed by loud whooping inhalations. According to a 1988 article in the *New York Times*, more than 250,000 cases of pertussis were reported annually in the United States in the 1930s. By 1987, the number of cases was down to 2,459, thanks to vaccines.

But there was a problem. The vaccines for whooping cough, though effective, were also dangerous and could cause serious side effects, including seizures and brain damage. Only about 1 in 100,000 patients suffered these side effects, but the number was high enough to alarm many physicians and parents. Public health officials still found the vaccines worthwhile and urged parents to have their children inoculated. Researchers went to work, however, and tried to develop new, risk-free vaccines.

Good news came in the early 1980s, when Japanese doctors reported that two new vaccines used in test experiments had proved safe and effective. These new vaccines, called acellular vaccines, marked a significant advance because they killed only some of the ingredients of the pertussis bacterium rather than the entire organism. By homing in on only a portion of the bacterium, these vaccines lowered the chances that the rest of the body might be adversely affected.

Test studies in Japan and in the United States confirmed that the new acellular vaccines might indeed eliminate pertussis as a serious childhood ailment. But further test results, released in 1988, showed, as the *Times* reported, "that [the new vaccines] are quite safe but not as effective as experts had hoped." These experiments were conducted over the course of several years by a Swedish research team, led by Dr. Lars O. Kallings of the National Bacteriological Laboratory in Stockholm. The team found that only two-thirds of the children given the vaccine recovered from pertussis, a percentage far lower than the 80% to 90% predicted by researchers. It seems more research is needed before a safe and effective vaccine for whooping cough is available.

This case illustrates that it takes a long time before a possible cure becomes reality, especially when researchers are dealing with elusive infectious agents. As recently as the 1950s, smallpox, polio, and tuberculosis seemed incurable ailments. By the year 2000, some of the most dreaded infectious diseases of today may also be tamed.

APPENDIX 1

TABLE 1

Infectious Diseases That Have a Vaccine		
Live Virus Vaccines	**Inactivated Virus Vaccines**	**Inactivated Bacterial Vaccines**
Measles	Hepatitis B	Cholera
Mumps	Influenza	Meningococcemia
Polio (given orally)	Rabies	Plague
Rubella (German measles)	Polio (given as a shot)	Pneumococcemia
Yellow Fever		Typhoid
		Pertussis (whooping cough)
Toxoids	**Other Bacterial Vaccines**	**Immunoglobulins***
Tetanus	Haemophilus influenzae type B1	Hepatitis A
Diphtheria		Hepatitis B
		Rabies
		Tetanus
		Varicella-zoster
		Measles

*Pooled antibodies for passive immunization

Table 2

Recommended Schedule of Immunizations for Infants and Children	
Age	**Vaccine**
2 months	DPT #1, OPV #1
4 months	DPT #2, OPV #2
6 months	DPT #3
15 months	MMR, DPT #4, OPV #3
24 months	HIB
4–6 years	DPT #5, OPV #4
14–16 years	Td
Abbreviations: DPT: diphtheria toxoid, pertussis vaccine, tetanus toxoid OPV: oral polio vaccine MMR: measles, mumps, and rubella vaccines HIB: Haemophilus influenzae type B Td: tetanus and diptheria toxoids (the adult-type dosage)	

APPENDIX 2:
FOR MORE INFORMATION

The following national associations and organizations can provide general information about the listed diseases. They can also offer names and phone numbers of local treatment centers.

AIDS

General Information Recording:
(800) 342-AIDS
Specific Information from the
United States Public Health
Service: (800) 447-AIDS
National Gay/Lesbian Crisis Line
(3:00 P.M.–9:00 P.M., EST): (800)
221-7044

ARTHRITIS

Arthritis Foundation
1314 Spring Street NW
Atlanta, GA 30309
(404) 872-7100

BONES AND JOINTS

American Association of
Orthopedic Medicine
c/o Kent Pomeroy, M.D.
926 East McDowell Road, #202
Phoenix, AZ 85006
(602) 254-5315

GASTROENTERITIS

American Digestive Disease Society
7720 Wisconsin Avenue NW
Bethesda, MD 20014
(301) 652-9293

American Gastroenterological
Association
6900 Grove Road
Thorofare, NJ 08086
(609) 848-1000

LEPROSY

American Leprosy Missions
One Broadway
Elmwood Park, NJ 07407
(201) 794-8650

VENEREAL DISEASE

American Venereal Disease
Association
Box 22349
San Diego, CA 92122
(619) 453-3238

National Sexually Transmitted
Diseases Hotline/American Social
Health Association
(800) 227-8922

RESPIRATORY DISEASES

American Lung Association
National Headquarters
1740 Broadway
New York, NY 10019
(212) 315-8700

Lung Hotline: (800) 222-LUNG
Colorado: (303) 398-1477

The following associations and hot lines can provide general information
about infectious diseases.

Centers for Disease Control
Department of Health and Human
   Services
Public Inquiries
Building 1, Room B63
1600 Clifton Road, NE
Atlanta, GA 30333
(404) 329-3534
(800) 342-7514

International Society on Infectious
   Diseases and Human Fertility
1430 Second Avenue
New York, NY 10021
(212) 774-5500

National Foundation for Infectious
   Diseases (NFID)
P.O. Box 42022
Washington, DC 20015
(301) 656-0003

National Institute of Allergy and
   Infectious Diseases(NIAID/NIH)
9000 Rockville Pike
Building 31, Room 7A32
Bethesda, MD 20892
(301) 496-5717

FURTHER READING

Bennett, L. Claire. *Communicable Diseases Handbook*. New York: Wiley, 1982.

Brettle, Raymond Patrick. *Infection and Communicable Diseases*. London: Heinemann, 1984.

Chase, Allan. *Magic Shots*. New York: Morrow, 1982.

Cherniak, Reuben M. *Respiration in Health and Diseases*. Philadelphia: Saunders, 1972.

Dowling, Harry Filmore. *Fighting Infection*. Cambridge: Harvard University Press, 1977.

Engleman, Ephraim P., and Milton Silverman. *The Book on Arthritis: A Guide for Patients and Their Families*. New York: Dutton, 1979.

Jones, Kenneth L., et al. *Communicable and Noncommunicable Disease*. New York: Harper & Row, 1975.

Kahn, Ada P. *Arthritis*. Chicago, IL: Contemporary Books, 1983.

Keating, Louise J., and Arthur J. Silvergleid, eds. *Hepatitis*. Chicago, IL: Academic Press, 1983.

Kittredge, Mary. *The Respiratory System*. New York: Chelsea House, 1989.

Kluger, Matthew J. *Fever*. Princeton, NJ: Princeton University Press, 1979.

Koop, C. Everett, M.D. *Surgeon General's Report on Acquired Immune Deficiency Syndrome*. Washington, DC: U.S. Department of Health and Human Services, 1987. (This can be obtained free of charge from InterAmerica Research, 1200E North Henry Street, Alexandria, VA 22314, Attention: Clint Jones)

Nourese, Alan E. *AIDS*. New York: Franklin Watts, 1986.

Silverstein, Alvin. *The Respiratory System*. Englewood Cliffs, NJ: Prentice-Hall, 1969.

Wedgood, Ralph J. *Infections in Children*. Philadelphia: Lippincott, 1982.

Wehrle, Paul F., and Franklin H. Top. *Communicable and Infectious Diseases*. St. Louis, MO: Mosby, 1981.

Zuckerman, Arie, and Colin Howard. *Hepatitis Viruses of Man*. Chicago, IL: Academic Press, 1982.

Krugman, Saul. *Infectious Diseases of Children*. St. Louis, MO: Mosby, 1981.

———. "Viral Hepatitis." Vol. 15 of *Major Problems in Internal Medicine*. Ann Arbor, MI: Books on Demand, 1982.

Nourese, Alan E. *AIDS*. New York: Franklin Watts, 1986.

Silverstein, Alvin. *The Respiratory System*. Englewood Cliffs, NJ: Prentice-Hall, 1969.

Wedgood, Ralph J. *Infections in Children*. Philadelphia: Lippincott, 1982.

Wehrle, Paul F., and Franklin H. Top. *Communicable and Infectious Diseases*. St. Louis, MO: Mosby, 1981.

Zuckerman, Arie, and Colin Howard. *Hepatitis Viruses of Man*. Chicago, IL: Academic Press, 1982.

GLOSSARY

active immunization type of immunity whereby the body is exposed to an antigen and, ideally, develops the appropriate antibody in response

AIDS acquired immune deficiency syndrome; a contagious defect of the immune system caused by a virus (HIV) and spread by contaminated blood, sexual contact, or nutritive fluids passed from a mother to a fetus; leaves people vulnerable to infections and certain types of cancer and is almost always fatal

antibiotic a substance derived from a mold or bacterium that inhibits the growth of bacteria and other microorganisms; used to combat infection caused by microorganisms

antibody one of several types of substances produced by the body to combat bacteria, viruses, and other foreign substances

antigen a bacteria, virus, or other foreign substance that causes the body to form an antibody

antisepsis the practice of cleaning areas of the body, usually the skin, where germs may flourish

asepsis creating a germ-free environment

bacteria unicellular organisms that lack a distinct nuclear membrane; some cause diseases that can be treated with antibiotics such as penicillin

bronchiolitis a viral infection of the lower respiratory tract, usually causing wheezing in young children or colds in older children

bronchitis an infection of the lower respiratory tract, striking when the large and small branches of the bronchial tree become inflamed and infected; more serious than bronchiolitis

Burkitt's lymphoma a tumor of the jaw associated with Epstein-Barr virus (EBV); most often found in African children

capsule an additional protective coating around the cell wall of some bacteria, possibly making them more resistant to attacks from the immune system

CBC complete blood count; a test that measures the number of red and white blood cells in a patient; used to diagnose various diseases, including mononucleosis

cell wall a protective coating, composed of sugar and protein molecules, that makes the outside of the cell rigid

chicken pox varicella; an infectious disease caused by the virus *Herpesvirus varicellae*, usually striking children under 10 between January and May; symptoms include general malaise, fever, and small, itchy red bumps that flatten, fill with clear fluid, and then break open within 24 hours

chlamydia the most common sexually transmitted disease; it can lead to pelvic inflammatory disease, which may cause sterility; treatable with antibiotics

congenital present from birth

croup laryngotracheobronchitis; a viral illness common among young children; usually caused by the parainfluenza viruses

cytoplasm the fluid filling the cell membrane; where ribosomes and the nuclear body are located

cytoplasmic membrane a semipermeable membrane made up of molecules of protein and of phospholipid; encloses individual cells

DNA deoxyribonucleic acid; genetic material, located in all cells as a double strand of paired nitrogenous bases, that contains the codes for an organism's inherited characteristics; most genes and chromosomes are made of DNA

enzyme a kind of protein that facilitates or triggers certain chemical or biological processes

epiglottitis inflammation and infection of the epiglottis, a life-threatening illness almost always caused by *Haemophilus influenzae* type B

EBV Epstein-Barr virus; the virus that causes infectious mononucleosis and other maladies

gastroenteritis inflammation of the stomach or intestines; caused by a variety of viral, bacterial, or parasitic infections

genital warts condyloma; fleshy growths occurring in and around the genitals and anus in both sexes; transmitted sexually by the human papilloma virus (HPV)

gonorrhea bacterially caused venereal disease, the second most common in the world; affects the genital mucous membranes; if treated early, antibiotics can be effective; if left untreated, serious complications may occur

Guillain-Barré syndrome an unusual condition associated with mononucleosis that seems to occur spontaneously, temporarily paralyzing some or all of the muscles in the patient's body

Hansen's disease leprosy; disease resulting from the invasion of *Mycobacterium leprae* into a person's skin and nerves, causing extensive lumps and severe nerve damage; many lepers lose fingers and toes because the nerve damage obstructs the sensation of pain from injuries such as cuts and burns, allowing infections to continue

hepatitis the inflammation and infection of the liver, caused by a wide variety of viral agents; hepatitis A is generally transmitted from person to person, while hepatitis B is generally transmitted by contact with blood

HIV human immunodeficiency virus; the virus that causes AIDS

herpesvirus a family of viruses containing large amounts of DNA; diseases caused by this family of viruses include herpes simplex, which causes painful sores on the mouth (simplex I) or on the anus and genitals (simplex II); the latter type can be passed on to a fetus

HVH *Herpesvirus hominis*; the virus that causes herpes simplex in humans

immunoglobulins globular proteins produced by the immune system to act as antibodies; immunoglobulins include types D, E, G, and M and type A, which is present in saliva, tears, and mucus

incubation period the interval between exposure to a disease and the appearance of symptoms

IV intravenous; the process of giving fluid or medication through a tube inserted into a vein

macrophage a white blood cell that captures and digests foreign bacteria

measles a disease caused by morbillivirus, transmitted from person to person by respiratory secretions; produces an illness characterized by fever, cough, runny nose, conjunctivitis, and a rash

meningitis an inflammation of the tissues or membranes covering the brain and spinal cord (the meninges)

mesosome a section of the cell membrane, pushed into the cytoplasm, that may be involved in the genetic process by helping one cell to divide in two

metaphysis the transitional part of a long bone; between the ossified section and the part that grows; it is where most bone infections begin

mumps endemic parotitis; an illness caused by the mumps virus, which produces inflammation of the parotid glands, located between the ear and the angle of the jaw

myocarditis infection of the heart muscle; can occur as a result of mononucleosis

nasopharyngeal carcinoma an EBV-associated cancer of the nose and throat, most commonly striking Chinese and Eskimo adults

normal flora any of the many microorganisms that live on the skin or in the respiratory, genitourinary, and gastrointestinal systems without causing infection

nuclear body the area of each cell wherein the genetic material, including DNA and RNA, is stored

osteomyelitis usually a childhood disease that can strike nearly any bone in the body, although it is primarily a disease of growing long bones; in most cases, an upper respiratory infection or a bacterial infection from the skin spreads to the bloodstream and is deposited in the metaphysis of a long bone, setting up a localized infection

otitis media an infection of the middle ear as a complication of an upper respiratory infection; most common among children

passive immunization type of immunity whereby physicians take antibodies from different people, pool them, and then give them to someone who has been exposed to an antigen but cannot produce a rapid response or any response at all

Pasteurella pestis the organism of plague, which multiplies in the victim's bloodstream and poisons the blood, thus causing death

pharyngitis sore throat, usually caused by a viral infection

plasma the clear, fluid part of blood that serves as a medium for the circulation of blood cells

pneumonia the inflammation and infection of the bronchial tree and the lung tissue; can be caused by viruses, bacteria, fungi, or *Mycoplasma pneumonia*

pus the yellowish white fluid composed of damaged tissue, microorganisms, and white blood cells, signaling infection

pyelonephritis an infection resulting from bacteria in the bladder that ascend the ureters and invade the kidneys

rheumatic fever inflammation and subsequent damage to heart valves; a possible complication of sinusitis, otitis media, or strep throat

RNA ribonucleic acid; genetic material, located in the nuclear body of some cells, structured like a single strand of DNA; the bases in RNA "mirror" those in DNA, enabling RNA to replicate its analogous DNA strand

ribosomes decoding structures, located in the cytoplasm, that translate DNA into the intermediary structure RNA

rubella German measles, an acute, infectious disease that can cause birth defects if the mother contracts it during pregnancy

Salmonella gastroenteritis-causing bacteria that live in poultry, eggs, and meat

septic arthritis an infection within the joint capsule that most commonly strikes children

shigella an invasive bacteria that causes dysentery

sinusitis inflammation and infection of the sinuses; a common complication of URI

smallpox a highly contagious disease caused by a virus of the *Poxviridae* or poxvirus family; the largest killer of children throughout Europe until the early 18th century; smallpox is now controlled by vaccinations

sputum mucus made up of saliva and discharges from the lining of the bronchial tree; can be the source of spreading certain infectious diseases if coughed up by an infected person

Staphylococcus aureus a type of bacteria that causes a short-lived but violent bacterial gastroenteritis, or food poisoning

STD sexually transmitted disease; includes AIDS, herpes simplex II, gonorrhea, chlamydia, and syphilis

TB tuberculosis; a respiratory ailment that damages many of the body's organs, particularly the lungs; carried through the bloodstream to the bones, the brain, and the urinary tract and spread by an infected person coughing up sputum

URI upper respiratory infection; any one of a variety of illnesses, also known as acute nasopharyngitis or the common cold

vaccine a substance made of a killed or weakened bacterium or virus; stimulates the body to create antibodies that increase an individual's immunity to a particular disease

virulence a bacteria's potential for infection

virus a minute acellular parasite composed of genetic matter (either DNA or RNA) called the core, a protein coat called the capsid, and an envelope around both core and capsid called the nucleocapsid; viruses have not clearly been classified as either living or nonliving; they can only reproduce within living host cells, which they destroy; known to cause such diseases as polio, measles, rabies, smallpox, and AIDS

white blood cell the type of blood cell that includes lymphocytes and polymorphonuclear cells and macrophages, which inactivate, "eat," or dissolve invading microorganisms

Yersinia pestis the bacterium that causes bubonic plague (usually transmitted from rat fleas to man) and pneumonic plague (usually transmitted from person to person by body lice)

INDEX

PICTURE CREDITS

Courtesy of Department of Library Services, American Museum of Natural History: p. 28; AP/Wide World Photos: p. 85; Dr. Edward J. Bottone, Microbiology Department, Mt. Sinai Hospital, New York: pp. 73, 74; Centers for Disease Control, Atlanta: pp. 46, 47, 59, 63, 82; Library of Congress: pp. 13, 20; Joan Liftin/Archive Pictures: p. 37; National Library of Medicine: pp. 15, 17, 19, 22, 23, 25, 33, 34, 39, 49, 61, 71; The Stock Market/Roy Morsch: p. 95; UPI/Bettmann Newsphotos: cover, pp. 42, 43; Original Art by Nisa Rauschenberg: pp. 27, 30, 44, 51, 52, 53, 55, 56, 67, 69, 75, 79, 81, 83, 86, 88

Laurel Shader, M.D., is a pediatrician practicing with Children's Medical Group, in Hamden, Connecticut, and a clinical instructor of pediatrics at the Yale University School of Medicine.

Jon Zonderman is an author and free-lance journalist who specializes in science, technology, and business. His book *Beyond the Crime Lab: The Science and Technology of Criminal Investigation* will be published later in 1989 by John Wiley & Sons.

Dale C. Garell, M.D., is medical director of California Childrens Services, Department of Health Services, County of Los Angeles. He is also clinical professor in the Department of Pediatrics and Family Medicine at the University of Southern California School of Medicine and Visiting associate clinical professor of maternal and child health at the University of Hawaii School of Public Health. From 1963 to 1974, he was medical director of the Division of Adolescent Medicine at Children's Hospital in Los Angeles. Dr. Garell has served as president of the Society for Adolescent Medicine, chairman of the youth committee of the American Academy of Pediatrics, and as a forum member of the White House Conference on Children (1970) and White House Conference on Youth (1971). He has also been a member of the editorial board of the *American Journal of Diseases of Children.*

C. Everett Koop, M.D., Sc.D., is Surgeon General, Deputy Assistant Secretary for Health, and Director of the Office of International Health of the U.S. Public Health Service. A pediatric surgeon with an international reputation, he was previously surgeon-in-chief of Children's Hospital of Philadelphia and professor of pediatric surgery and pediatrics at the University of Pennsylvania. Dr. Koop is the author of more than 175 articles and books on the practice of medicine. He has served as surgery editor of the *Journal of Clinical Pediatrics* and editor-in-chief of the *Journal of Pediatric Surgery.* Dr. Koop has received nine honorary degrees and numerous other awards, including the Denis Brown Gold Medal of the British Association of Paediatric Surgeons, the William E. Ladd Gold Medal of the American Academy of Pediatrics, and the Copernicus Medal of the Surgical Society of Poland. He is a Chevalier of the French Legion of Honor and a member of the Royal College of Surgeons, London.

616.9   Shader, Laurel

Shader   Mononucleosis and
          other infectious
          dieseases

$18.95   019113

		DATE		
NOV 1 8 2005				

© THE BAKER & TAYLOR CO.